A GARDENER'S GUIDE TO

Ferns, Palms & Climbers

Editor Alan Toogood

Series Editor Graham Strong

MURDOCH BOOKS

Murdoch Books UK Ltd, Ferry House, 51–57 Lacy Road, Putney, London SW15 1PR

CONTENTS

LEFT: The delicate flowers of Jasminum polyanthum *(jasmine) here provide
a perfumed welcome for visitors and family alike.*

GROWING FERNS

Ferns and fern allies come in many forms but they all reproduce from spores rather than seeds. There are over 10,000 fern species, and while the majority of them occur in humid tropical and subtropical zones, there are also ferns native to cool and cold climates.

Ferns are very old – fossil ferns date back many millions of years – but the height of their popularity was probably during Victorian times, when even modest gardens had a 'fernery'. In general, ferns like good light but not direct sun. Most prefer a moist atmosphere and shelter from strong, drying winds, although some species grow in fairly exposed places, and they need some moisture around their roots at all times, but not waterlogged conditions.

Ferns, which may be evergreen or herbaceous, are divided into two groups: terrestrial (ground growing) and epiphytic (growing on trees). The latter, mainly tropical and subtropical kinds, are not parasites but simply use trees for support. The hardy ferns considered here are terrestrial and are grown like any other garden plant.

LEFT: Ferns more than make up for their lack of bright colours with their stunning forms and subtly textured foliage.

USES IN GARDENS

Ferns thrive in groups. Planting a collection of ferns in dense communities improves their growing conditions by raising atmospheric humidity and providing shade and protection. Humus derived from the breakdown of old fronds (leaves), if they are not removed, tends to build up in the soil, helping to keep it moisture retentive.

A corner of a garden planted with ferns can be just as attractive as areas with flowering plants. If the various heights, textures and shades of green of the ferns are considered, a beautiful picture can be created. Provided the climate is suitable for them, tall *Dicksonia* tree ferns can be underplanted with smaller ferns, such as *Athyrium filix-femina* (Lady fern), *Blechnum* species (Hard ferns), *Dryopteris* (Buckler ferns), *Matteuccia struthiopteris* (Ostrich or shuttlecock fern) and *Polystichum* (Shield ferns).

Spring is generally a peak time for ferns when they are unfurling their new bright green fronds, although they also look good in summer. If grouped with spring-flowering plants such as woodland perennials they can create a wonderfully 'fresh' atmosphere, creating a scene reminiscent of lush woodland dells or even jungle. The evergreen ferns will look good all year round whereas the herbaceous kinds die down in autumn, but even then the dead fronds of some can still look good when they turn golden brown and add to the general autumn display.

Moist shady spots

Any shady spot in the garden is suitable for ferns, provided the soil remains moist but does not become waterlogged. For example, the shade may be created by the house or other buildings. The area in front of the north-facing side of a shed or garage is in shade, the ideal place for a collection of ferns. Or the shade may be cast by a tree or shrub, in which case it may be dappled, providing very acceptable conditions for these plants.

Ferneries

Ferneries, which are collections of ferns, were very popular in the Victorian period. With the general renewal of interest in ferns, ferneries are now coming back into fashion. In Victorian times the ferns were grown among rocks and even tree stumps and pieces of tree root to create naturalistic effects, creating an romantic setting that harked to far-off corners of the British Empire. This is a perfectly acceptable way to grow them today. Also in Victorian times a grotto (a small artificial picturesque cave) might have had a fernery at its entrance.

When choosing ferns for a collection make sure they are all suited to the same amount of shade and soil conditions (see recommended ferns from pages 12 to 23).

Shrub borders

Perhaps a more widely used way to display ferns today is in borders of deciduous and evergreen shrubs, as the two groups of plants complement each other admirably, being so different in shape and texture. To create a spring picture try grouping herbaceous ferns such as *Athyrium filix-femina* (Lady fern), *Dryopteris filix-mas* (Male fern), *Matteuccia struthiopteris* (Ostrich fern) or *Onoclea sensibilis* (Sensitive fern) around spring-flowering shrubs, such as rhododendrons and azaleas (for acid soils only), magnolias, *Corylopsis pauciflora*, *Spiraea arguta* or *Amelanchier lamarckii* (Juneberry). For winter interest in the garden mass plant evergreen ferns, such as *Asplenium scolopendrium* (Hart's

FERNS ARE USED HERE to add depth of texture to this casual planting. Their tall arching fronds provide a pleasing highlight to the general mass of smaller plants, while their general appearance contributes to the overall lushness intended for this area of the garden.

A SMALL POND is fringed with ferns and other plants to create a picture that looks completely natural. Water iris grow in the pond, while the edging plants, including broad-leaved bergenias, are all types that love plenty of shade and moisture.

tongue fern) and *Blechnum species* (Hard ferns) around and under winter-flowering shrubs including the evergreen *Viburnum tinus* (Laurustinus), *Hamamelis* (Witch hazels) with their spidery yellow or orange flowers on bare twigs, evergreen *Mahonia japonica* and the deciduous, fragrant *Daphne mezereum* (Mezereon).

Woodland gardens

A woodland garden might sound too ambitious for an ordinary town or suburban plot, but this need not be the case. A group of just two or three trees, or even a single small tree, is sufficient to create such a desirable feature. White-stemmed birches, such as *Betula pendula* (Silver birch) or *B. utilis* var. *jacquemontii* (Himalayan birch) are ideal for the purpose, casting light, dappled shade, under which a wide range of woodland shrubs, perennials and bulbs can be grown, with ferns mixed in among them. A particular favourite for woodland gardens is *Matteuccia struthiopteris* (Ostrich fern) with upright 'shuttlecocks' of fresh, pale green fronds. Try grouping this plant with spring- and early summer-flowering woodland primulas, such as *Primula denticulata* (Drumstick primrose) and *P. japonica* (Japanese primrose), *Meconopsis betonicifolia* (Himalayan blue poppy), spring-flowering shrubs such as rhododendrons and azaleas (for acid soils only) and *Acer palmatum* cultivars (Japanese maples) which, like ferns, produce superb spring foliage.

Poolside

Poolside plantings can include various ferns which do not mind an open sunny position with moist soil. One of the best for this purpose is *Osmunda regalis* (Royal fern) which

DIFFERENT SHADES OF GREEN, with ferns used for the lightest shade, provide the perfect colour base for these rhododendron blooms.

relishes wet soil. Its upright bright green fronds make a
charming foil for flowering poolside perennials such as
astilbes with feathery plumes of flowers, and primulas
including *P. florindae* (Giant cowslip).

CULTIVATION

Aspect
In the main ferns like to grow in a position sheltered from
cold drying winds, with unbroken shade or dappled shade
cast by trees and shrubs. There are a few exceptions to this
rule, as some ferns, such as the dwarf *Asplenium* species,
are to be found in open, exposed positions in their natural
habitat. In cultivation these species would be quite happy
growing on an exposed and sunny rock garden.

Soil
Most ferns are able to cope with a wide range of garden
soils. The ideal, however, is a well-drained, well-aerated,
but moisture-retentive loam containing a large amount
of humus. Most ferns will be happy in the full range of
soil, whether alkaline, neutral or acid conditions. Some,
though, such as *Blechnum* species, definitely need acid soil
and would fail in limy or alkaline soils. Some ferns, such
as *Asplenium* species (Spleenworts), will tolerate drier
conditions than most others.
 Although most ferns like moist conditions, they
will not tolerate soils that are prone to waterlogging.
Heavy clay or other soil that is prone to lying wet for
long periods can be improved by digging in copious
amounts of grit or coarse sand (choose those suitable for
horticultural use) to open it up and improve drainage
and aeration. All soils, especially those prone to drying
out such as sandy types, will benefit from the addition
of bulky organic matter during digging to help them
retain moisture during dry periods. Ground or chipped
composted bark, or leafmould, are ideal for ferns, but
garden compost is also suitable. Never use animal
manures as these are too rich for ferns, even when they
have been well rotted.

Planting
Ferns may be planted at any time of year if they are
bought in containers. A good time, though, is in early
spring just before they start into growth, as the soil is
warming up and well charged with moisture. Then they
will establish really quickly. When removing plants from
their pots, do not disturb the roots. Plant to the same
depth so that the crown is at soil level – never plant ferns
so that the crown is below the soil. Water young plants
well during dry weather to encourage them to establish
quickly. Once planted, ferns should be left alone for as
long as possible as they do not like root disturbance.

Care
Ferns need very little in the way of maintenance.
Mulching around them with chipped or ground
composted bark, leafmould, coir or garden compost will
keep the soil cool and help to retain moisture during
warm dry weather, and prevent weed growth. Mulch is
best applied in the spring just before ferns start into
growth. The soil should be moist and weed free when it is
applied. Spread the mulching material over the soil
surface as evenly as possible, to a depth of 5–8cm (2–3in).
Replace it as required. Bark is the longest lasting material
and should remain effective for several years.

THE SWIRLING, pale green fronds of Asplenium scolopendrium
'Crispum' demonstrate the astonishing variety of ferns.

*FERNS PLAY AN IMPORTANT part of this well-structured bank
of foliage, providing a lush backdrop for the foreground plants.*

A TYPICAL FERN SETTING. A shady spot with moist but not sodden soil provides the perfect habitat for ferns. Here they are used as groundcover with other shade-loving plants, each adding to the intended natural woodland air of this secluded corner of the garden.

Ferns will need a bit of attention during long periods of dry weather. If the soil starts to dry out, ferns will need watering. It is best to give them a good soaking, say once or twice a week, rather than frequent 'light showers'. During very hot breezy weather when humidity is low, ferns will also appreciate being sprayed overhead daily with a garden sprinkler. A permanent watering system, such as seep hoses laid between plants, is worth considering to quickly provide constant soil moisture and cut down on watering time.

Ferns should be fed during the spring and summer when they are in growth, but avoid overdoing it as they do not like a rich diet. Organic fertilizers are recommended. A slow-release fertilizer, such as blood, fish and bone, could be applied in spring just as growth is starting, lightly forking it into the soil under the mulch. This will last the ferns for the entire growing season. Alternatively the plants could be given weak liquid seaweed fertilizer every four weeks or so, but this is more time consuming.

Dead and dying fronds are best removed at some stage. You may like to leave them over winter as often they turn a pleasing golden brown colour and add to the winter scene. Also they help to protect the crown of the plants from severe weather. They can then be removed in the spring just before growth starts, by cutting them off close to the crown of the plant with secateurs.

AMID A SEA OF BLUEBELLS, these clumps of ferns lend a striking structural dimension to this wild garden area.

PROPAGATION

Division

Division is the easiest method of propagating most ferns. It may be as simple as cutting off a section of creeping stem or rhizome that has some roots attached and planting it elsewhere to the same depth.

Clump-forming ferns, which include the majority of hardy kinds, can have their crowns divided into portions in early to mid-spring. Lift the clump carefully with a spade, aiming to avoid root damage. Some large clumps may be difficult to pull apart by hand, so thrust two forks back to back through the centre and prise the handles apart. Repeat this with the two portions to give you four smaller clumps for replanting. Each portion for replanting must have plenty of roots and at least one crown with growth buds. Replant to the same depth as before.

Growing from bulbils

Some ferns, such as several species of *Polystichum* or Shield ferns, produce 'bulbils' or tiny plantlets on the fronds in late summer and autumn. As the fronds age, the weight of the newly developing plantlets forces them to the ground where the plantlets take root. Alternatively pin an old frond to the ground with wire V-shaped pins, to allow the plantlets to develop roots. You could also carefully remove mature fronds and pin them to the surface of soilless seed

compost in a seed tray until the plantlets are established. Enclose the tray in a plastic bag and keep it in a warm, light but shaded place. Pot the small plants into 7cm (3in) pots when large enough to handle easily.

Growing from spores

Spores, the fern equivalent of seeds, are found on the underside of fronds. They may occur in masses all over the frond, in lines, or around the margins of leaflets.

Raising ferns from spores in an artificial environment is not easy. It can take 18–24 months from sowing to planting out. But the ferns themselves are usually obliging, and if you have provided optimum conditions you may find colonies of youngsters, produced from spores, appearing around parent plants.

It is sometimes difficult to know when spores are mature or if they have already been shed. They normally appear in late summer. Unripe spore cases are green or light yellow, but turn dark brown, orange or blue-grey when ripe. To collect spores, place a frond in a paper bag, keep it in a warm room and wait for a few days for the spores to be shed. They look like fine brown dust.

Fern spores can be sown on many types of growing media, but whatever is used it must first be sterilized, together with the containers, to kill harmful organisms and moss spores. Soilless seed compost is suitable. Finely shredded sphagnum moss or coarse washed sand are often

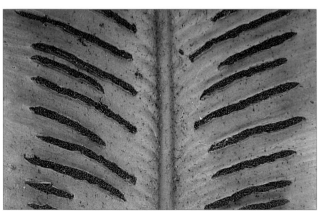

THE RIPE SPORE cases of this Asplenium scolopendrium *(Hart's tongue fern) are arranged in parallel lines radiating from the vein.*

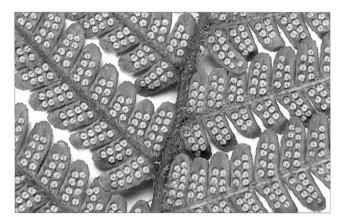

DRYOPTERIS WALLICHIANA *(Wallich's wood fern) has spore cases arranged in small dots – these ones are not yet ripe.*

THE TWISTING FRONDS of Polypodium vulgare *(Common polypody) are home to the plant's slightly elongated spore cases.*

THESE MORE RANDOM spore cases lend Dryopteris affinis Crispa Group *a hint of mauve, attractive in large plantings.*

FERN LIFE CYCLE

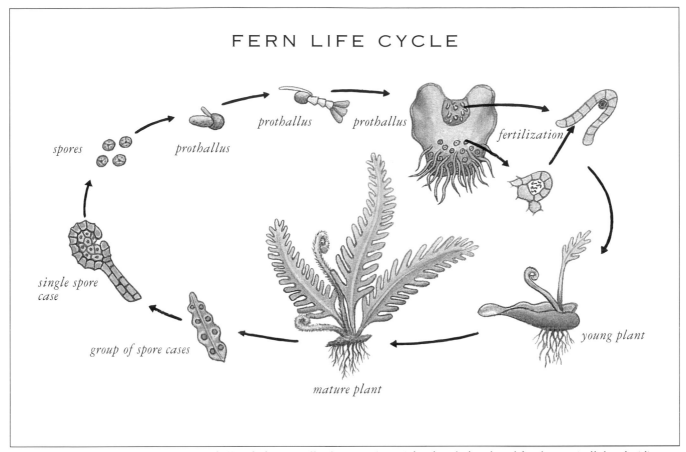

spores

prothallus

prothallus

prothallus

fertilization

single spore case

group of spore cases

mature plant

young plant

THE SPORES OF A FERN develop into prothalli, which are usually about 1cm (⅓in). These have both male and female parts (called antheridium and archegonia respectively). After self-fertilization the new plant begins to grow from the prothallus.

used, either alone or mixed together. Crushed brick or terracotta pots, used alone or mixed with coarse washed sand, are also suitable.

The most common propagation containers are small seed trays, pans or pots. First sterilize them with boiling water. Then fill with the growing medium and sterilize this by pouring boiling water over it until it runs out of the bottom of the container. Enclose in a plastic bag while cooling off to prevent contamination. Make sure the surface of the growing medium is smooth and level, then sow the spores thinly on it. Cover the container immediately with clear glass or enclose in a plastic bag, then stand it in a closed propagating case in a warm, light, but shaded place such as a greenhouse. Germinate spores at 15–20°C (59–68°F). Ensure the growing medium is kept moist at all times, using tepid, boiled water.

After several months the surface of the growing medium will be covered with a green moss-like growth, the prothalli. Lift out small squares of this growth and replant them on the surface of sterilized soilless seed compost in small seed trays or pans. Gently press them onto the surface. Spray them with water to settle them in, then enclose the containers in clear plastic bags and return them to the propagating case. Keep moist and as soon as plantlets have developed pot them individually into cell trays or small pots of soilless potting compost. Pot on as necessary until large enough for planting out. Alternatively, transplanting can be delayed until tiny fronds appear on the prothalli.

EPIPHYTIC FERNS are those that naturally grow on trees or other elevated areas. They can be used to interesting effect in the garden.

ADIANTUM
Maidenhair fern

THE SOFT, CASCADING FOLIAGE of Maidenhair fern has almost universal appeal. The very fine forms are the hardest to grow.

ADIANTUM PEDATUM (Five-fingered maidenhair) is a hardy fern that can be used in a border with partial shade.

FEATURES

Partial shade

The adiantums are dainty low-growing ferns with rounded or diamond-shaped leaf segments, and the fronds are often carried on attractive, wiry black stems. Many of the maidenhair ferns will not tolerate frost but there are several frost-hardy species which make delightful additions to shady parts of the garden. They are a good choice for woodland gardens or shrub borders, associating well with small spring-flowering perennials. The well-known *Adiantum pedatum* is herbaceous but many other species are evergreen, including *A. venustum*, another popular kind, whose new fronds, which are produced in late winter and early spring, are pinky bronze.

ADIANTUM AT A GLANCE

Dwarf evergreen and herbaceous ferns with dainty foliage on black stems. Hardy to −15°C (5°F).

		COMPANION PLANTS
JAN	/	
FEB	/	Astilbe
MAR	planting	Bergenia
APR	planting	Corylopsis
MAY	foliage	Hosta
JUN	foliage	*Hyacinthoides non-scripta*
JULY	foliage	Primula
AUG	foliage	Pulmonaria
SEP	/	Rhododendron
OCT	/	Rodgersia
NOV	/	
DEC	/	

CONDITIONS

Aspect   Partial shade is best, such as the dappled shade provided by trees and shrubs.

Site   Moist but well-drained, reasonably fertile soil, rich in humus such as provided by leafmould.

GROWING METHOD

Propagation   The easiest method of propagation is to divide established clumps in early spring just as the plants are coming into growth. Plant 30cm (12in) apart. Adiantums can also be grown from spores but this is a more challenging method.

Watering   Water freely during dry weather.

Feeding   Apply a slow-release organic fertilizer in the spring just as growth is starting.

Problems   No pest and disease problems with maidenhair ferns grown out of doors.

FOLIAGE DISPLAY

Season   The optimum display period is in the spring when new fronds are unfurling, but these ferns also look good throughout summer. The evergreen species will provide interest all year round.

GENERAL CARE

Requirements Cut off any dead fronds in spring just before growth starts. Provide a mulch in spring before the plants start into growth.

ASPLENIUM
Hart's tongue fern

ASPLENIUM SCOLOPENDRIUM 'Angustatum' has attractive glossy fronds with frilly edges, making it a garden favourite.

THE SNAKING A. s. 'Angustatum' make a powerful architectural impact in any garden setting, formal or informal.

FEATURES

Partial shade

The Hart's tongue fern (*Asplenium scolopendrium*) is quite distinct from many other ferns with its undivided, strap-shaped fronds which are produced in a shuttlecock formation. These are a bright, fresh green, especially when young. In the wild it is very widely distributed, from Europe, through western Asia to North America, where it is often found growing on shady banks. It makes excellent ground cover in a shrub border or woodland garden if planted in bold groups or drifts around shrubs. This especially hardy fern associates particularly well with trees and shrubs and is quite drought tolerant. There are numerous cultivars available that are also worth growing.

ASPLENIUM AT A GLANCE

A dwarf evergreen fern with unusual strap-shaped fronds. Very easily grown. Hardy to –15°C (5°F).

JAN	foliage 🌿	RECOMMENDED VARIETIES
FEB	foliage 🌿	*Asplenium scolopendrium*
MAR	planting ✋	Crispum Group
APR	planting ✋	A. s. Cristatum Group
MAY	foliage 🌿	A. s. Marginatum Group
JUN	foliage 🌿	A. s. Undulatum Group
JULY	foliage 🌿	
AUG	foliage 🌿	
SEP	foliage 🌿	
OCT	foliage 🌿	
NOV	foliage 🌿	
DEC	foliage 🌿	

CONDITIONS

Aspect Prefers a position in partial shade, such as the dappled shade cast by trees and shrubs.

Site The soil should be moisture-retentive but well-drained and rich in humus. Alkaline soil is preferred although this fern also grows in acid conditions.

GROWING METHOD

Propagation The best method is to divide established plants in the spring just before they start into growth. Plant 45–60cm (18–24in) apart. Can also be raised from spores but this is more challenging.

Watering Water freely during dry weather.

Feeding Apply an organic slow-release fertilizer in the spring just as plants are starting into growth.

Problems During wet winters a rust disease may appear on the leaves. Cut off badly affected leaves.

FOLIAGE DISPLAY

Season This fern looks good all the year round but is at its best in spring when the plant is producing its new fronds.

GENERAL CARE

Requirements Cut off any dead fronds in spring just before growth starts. Provide a mulch in spring before the plants start into growth.

ATHYRIUM FILIX-FEMINA
Lady fern

THE FRONDS of Athyrium filix-femina *(Lady fern) are made up of many miniature leaflets, giving the plant a distinctive appearance.*

FROM A DISTANCE the individual appearance of A. filix-femina *can be seen. An adaptable plant, it will tolerate a range of settings.*

FEATURES

Shade

The Lady fern is probably one of the most widely grown ferns. It has upright, lance-shaped, pale green pinnate fronds, carried in a shuttlecock formation. It is also one of the taller ferns, the fronds reaching a height of 1.2m (4ft) when the plant is growing in optimum conditions. In the wild the Lady fern is very widely spread throughout the northern hemisphere. Suitable for any shady part of the garden – fernery, shrub border or woodland garden – it looks best when planted in a group of several plants and it associates especially well with spring-flowering shrubs.

ATHYRIUM AT A GLANCE

A very popular tall herbaceous fern with upright, very 'ferny' light green fronds. Hardy to –30°C (–22°F).

		RECOMMENDED VARIETIES
JAN	/	*Athyrium filix-femina*
FEB	/	Cristatum Group
MAR	planting 🖉	A. f. Cruciatum Group
APR	planting 🖉	A. f. 'Frizelliae'
MAY	foliage 🍂	A. f. 'Minutissimum'
JUN	foliage 🍂	A. f. Plumosum Group
JULY	foliage 🍂	
AUG	foliage 🍂	
SEP	/	
OCT	/	
NOV	/	
DEC	/	

CONDITIONS

Aspect This fern is best sited in a position with unbroken shade, with good shelter from cold and drying winds.

Site Best grown in neutral to acid soil that is also moisture retentive, reasonably fertile and rich in humus, such as provided by leafmould or composted ground or shredded bark.

GROWING METHOD

Propagation Lift and divide established plants in early to mid-spring. Then replant the divisions 60–90cm (24–36in) apart. The fern often freely propagates itself from spores under optimum conditions.

Watering Water the plants freely in dry weather.

Feeding Apply an organic slow-release fertilizer in the spring just as plants are starting into growth.

Problems This fern is not troubled by pests and disease.

FOLIAGE DISPLAY

Season The Lady fern is particularly attractive in spring as the new fronds are unfurling.

GENERAL CARE

Requirements Cut off the dead fronds just before the plants start into growth in the spring. Provide a mulch in spring before growth gets under way.

BLECHNUM
Hard fern

THE FRONDS *of* Blechnum chilense. *This species makes a fine architectural plant, with arching fronds reaching above smaller plants.*

BLECHNUM PENNA-MARINA *is an attractive dwarf variety that is at its best when planted as groundcover in large colonies.*

FEATURES

Shade

Blechnums are a large group of ferns found in various parts of the world from the tropics to temperate regions. They have attractive pinnate, leathery, ladderlike and often dark green fronds. Among the most popular species are *Blechnum chilense*, one of the taller species at 90cm (3ft); *B. penna-marina*, a dwarf with strap shaped fronds that are red-green when they unfurl; and *B. spicant*, another dwarf species, with fronds growing to 30cm (12in). The Hard ferns are ideal for shrub borders and woodland gardens and the dwarf species can also be recommended for rock gardens. The dwarf kinds also make very good all year round ground cover if they are mass planted.

BLECHNUM AT A GLANCE

Mainly dwarf evergreen ferns with pinnate fronds, suited to various garden situations. Hardy to −15°C (5°F).

		COMPANION PLANTS
JAN	foliage	Astilbe
FEB	foliage	Bergenia
MAR	planting	Corylopsis
APR	planting	Hosta
MAY	foliage	*Hyacinthoides non-scripta*
JUN	foliage	Primula
JULY	foliage	Pulmonaria
AUG	foliage	Rhododendron
SEP	foliage	Rodgersia
OCT	foliage	
NOV	foliage	
DEC	foliage	

CONDITIONS

Aspect Hard ferns can be grown either in partial or complete shade and they will also tolerate quite deep shade.

Site These ferns will only thrive in an acid or lime-free soil, which must also be moisture-retentive and rich in humus.

GROWING METHOD

Propagation Division of established plants in early to mid-spring is the usual method. Replant about 45cm (18in) apart.Propagation from spores is possible but more of a challenge.

Watering These ferns needs to be kept well watered during dry weather.

Feeding A slow-release organic fertilizer applied in spring just as growth is starting will keep the plants going for a year.

Problems There are no problems from pests and diseases.

FOLIAGE DISPLAY

Season These ferns are evergreen so they look good all year round. But as with all ferns, the young fronds in spring are particularly welcome and they retain their fresh look all summer.

GENERAL CARE

Requirements Remove dead fronds in the spring just before plants start into growth and at the same time provide a mulch.

DICKSONIA ANTARCTICA
Soft tree fern

THE BROAD, SPREADING CROWN of this Dicksonia antarctica looks magnificent as it grows out in dappled sunlight.

THIS SPECIES of fern has a very upright habit. Here it grows in a sheltered courtyard teamed with rhododendrons and potted kumquat.

FEATURES

Shade

This is one of the tallest ferns for the garden but, being a native of Australia, is only suitable for mild climates. It is slow growing but eventually forms a thick fibrous trunk with a canopy of large pinnate fronds at the top – in large plants these can grow to a length of 3m (10ft). The Soft tree fern is a fine specimen plant for sheltered woodland conditions, and a group of three or more is impressive. However, be warned, large plants are very expensive. Small plants are also available for those with plenty of patience.

DICKSONIA AT A GLANCE

An impressive, tall, evergreen, tree-like fern for the woodland garden, but only in mild areas. Hardy to –5°C (23°F).

		COMPANION PLANTS
JAN	foliage	Acer palmatum
FEB	foliage	Camellia
MAR	planting	Corylopsis
APR	planting	Fothergilla
MAY	foliage	Magnolia
JUN	foliage	Photinia
JULY	foliage	Pieris
AUG	foliage	Rhododendron
SEP	foliage	
OCT	foliage	
NOV	foliage	
DEC	foliage	

CONDITIONS

Aspect The soft tree fern needs to be grown in partial or full shade and in a position sheltered from cold drying winds. Wind can damage and 'scorch' the fronds.

Site The soil must be acid or lime-free, moisture-retentive and rich in humus.

GROWING METHOD

Propagation This is not really feasible for home gardeners. Like all ferns, it can be raised from spores but this is a very slow method.

Watering During hot, dry weather water the plant well and also spray the trunk daily with water.

Feeding Apply an organic slow-release fertilizer in the spring.

Problems There are no problems from pests and diseases.

FOLIAGE DISPLAY

Season Although it is evergreen, this tree fern looks its best in spring and summer. In winter fronds can be damaged by hard frosts.

GENERAL CARE

Requirements In spring cut off any dead fronds close to the trunk. Apply a mulch of organic matter in spring to provide humus and to help retain soil moisture.

DRYOPTERIS AFFINIS
Golden male fern

SHOWING OFF its symmetry, this frond of Dryopteris affinis *demonstrates the upright habit of this pleasing plant.*

A DENSE MASS of fronds reaching up out of the undergrowth are characteristic of the popular D. affinis, a native of Europe.

FEATURES

Partial shade

This is a very popular fern with lance-shaped pinnate fronds carried in a shuttlecock arrangement. The fronds can grow up to 90cm (36in) in height. They are pale green when newly emerged in spring and have attractive, scaly, gold-brown midribs. The fronds turn to deep green in summer and generally stay green all through the winter. This versatile fern associates well with a wide range of hardy perennials and shrubs. Try planting it around evergreen shrubs such as hollies and mahonias for a pleasing winter effect.

DRYOPTERIS A GLANCE

An easily grown fern with highly attractive, evergreen pinnate fronds.
Hardy to –15°C (5°F)

JAN	foliage	RECOMMENDED VARIETIES
FEB	foliage	*Dryopteris affinis* Crispa
MAR	planting	Group
APR	planting	*D. a.* 'Crispa Gracilis'
MAY	foliage	*D. a.* 'Cristata'
JUN	foliage	*D. a.* 'Cristata Angustata'
JULY	foliage	*D. a.* 'Polydactyla
AUG	foliage	Mapplebeck'
SEP	foliage	
OCT	foliage	
NOV	foliage	
DEC	foliage	

CONDITIONS

Aspect   Grow this fern in partial shade. The dappled shade provided by trees is ideal. The site should also be sheltered from cold winds.

Site   The soil needs to be moisture-retentive and rich in humus.

GROWING METHOD

Propagation   Division is the easiest method. Divide established clumps in early to mid-spring and replant 90cm (36in) apart. It can also be propagated from spores and may increase naturally by this method.

Watering   Water well when the weather is dry.

Feeding   Apply an organic slow-release fertilizer in spring just as growth is starting.

Problems   There are no problems from pests or diseases.

FOLIAGE DISPLAY

Season   This is an evergreen fern so it will provide interest all the year round. However it is at its best in spring and summer.

GENERAL CARE

Requirements Cut off any dead or tatty-looking fronds in the spring and apply a mulch of organic matter to help maintain moist, cool conditions.

DRYOPTERIS FILIX-MAS
Male fern

A FAMILIAR SIGHT in European woodland, a swathe of Dryopteris filix-mas *makes a dense and lush-looking garden feature.*

D. FILIX-MAS *is similar in appearance and growth habit to its relative* D. affinis, *but has fewer scales on its midribs.*

FEATURES

Partial shade

A large clump-forming fern with pinnate, lance-shaped fronds which can grow up to 1.2m (4ft) in height in optimum conditions. The fronds are mid-green in colour and have green midribs. This is a popular, easily grown fern which is suitable for shrub and mixed borders, woodland gardens and ferneries. It makes a good companion for trees, shrubs, and hardy shade-loving perennials of all kinds. The Male fern looks most impressive planted as a large colony, say a group of three to five plants, if space permits. Try grouping it with drifts of candelabra primulas for a stunning summer effect.

DRYOPTERIS AT A GLANCE

A large herbaceous fern with mid-green pinnate foliage and suitable for all shady parts of the garden.Hardy to –15°C (5°F).

		RECOMMENDED VARIETIES
JAN	/	*Dryopteris filix-mas* 'Barnesii'
FEB	/	D. f. 'Crispa Cristata'
MAR	planting 🖐	D. f. 'Cristata'
APR	planting 🖐	D. f. 'Grandiceps Wills'
MAY	foliage 🌿	D. f. 'Linearis'
JUN	foliage 🌿	D. f. 'Linearis Polydactyla'
JULY	foliage 🌿	
AUG	foliage 🌿	
SEP	/	
OCT	/	
NOV	/	
DEC	/	

CONDITIONS

Aspect This fern will thrive in partial shade. Dappled shade is particularly good, such as provided by trees or large shrubs. Ensure shelter from cold drying winds which can damage and 'scorch' the fronds, particularly young soft ones.

Site A soil which is rich in humus and moisture-retentive is recommended.

GROWING METHOD

Propagation Divide established clumps in early to mid-spring and replant 90cm (36in) apart. This fern may also increase naturally from spores – much easier than trying to raise them yourself

Watering During dry weather plants will appreciate regular and copious watering.

Feeding Apply an organic slow release fertilizer in spring as fronds are starting to appear.

Problems This fern is not troubled by pests and diseases.

FOLIAGE DISPLAY

Season The Male fern looks its best in spring and summer. The new fronds are particularly appealing.

GENERAL CARE

Requirements Cut down dead fronds in spring just before growth starts. Mulch with organic matter to maintain cool moist soil conditions.

MATTEUCCIA
Ostrich fern

THESE STERILE FRONDS of Matteuccia struthiopteris *surround the smaller fertile fronds, which appear in the late summer.*

A PAIR OF LIGHT green sterile M. struthiopteris *fronds. The smaller fertile fronds form the centre of the plant and produce spores.*

FEATURES

Partial shade

Matteuccia struthiopteris forms a real shuttlecock shape and its alternative name is Shuttlecock fern. The stiff, slightly angled, pinnate, lance-shaped fronds are light green and attain a height of at least 1.2m (4ft). Fertile spore-bearing fronds appear in late summer and remain throughout winter. It spreads by creeping stems or rhizomes which form new 'shuttlecocks' around the parent plant. In the wild this fern is widespread throughout Europe, eastern Asia and North America. One of the best choices for a woodland garden or shrub border, it also looks good by the side of a pool provided there is sufficient shade.

MATTEUCCIA AT A GLANCE

A large, handsome shuttlecock-shaped fern, this plant is especially beautiful in spring. Hardy to −15°C (5°F).

		COMPANION PLANTS
JAN	/	*Acer palmatum*
FEB	/	Camellia
MAR	planting 🖐	Corylopsis
APR	planting 🖐	Fothergilla
MAY	foliage 🍃	Magnolia
JUN	foliage 🍃	Meconopsis
JULY	foliage 🍃	Photinia
AUG	foliage 🍃	Pieris
SEP	/	Primula
OCT	/	Rhododendron
NOV	/	
DEC	/	

CONDITIONS

Aspect Suitable for dappled shade as cast by deciduous trees, or for partial unbroken shade.

Site The soil should be neutral or slightly acid, moisture-retentive yet well-drained and rich in humus.

GROWING METHOD

Propagation The easiest method is to divide established plants in early to mid spring. Replant the divisions 90cm (3ft) apart to give them room to develop. The offsets produced by the rhizomes can be removed and replanted elsewhere. Can also be raised from spores, but this is more challenging.

Watering Feeding Keep plants well watered during dry weather. Apply an organic slow-release fertilizer in spring just as growth is commencing.

Problems There are no problems from pests and diseases.

FOLIAGE DISPLAY

Season This fern is really stunning in the spring with its new fresh green fronds. They remain in good condition throughout the summer.

GENERAL CARE

Requirements Cut off the dead fronds in spring before new ones start unfurling and provide a mulch of organic matter.

ONOCLEA SENSIBILIS
Sensitive fern

THE ATTRACTIVE FORMS of these Onoclea sensibilis *fronds make a fine addition to a border, providing gentle sculptural interest.*

THE GENTLY RIPPLING edges of O. sensibilis *are what give this fern its highly distinctive appearance.*

FEATURES

Partial shade

The wide lance-shaped or even triangular fronds of the Sensitive fern start erect then arch over. They are pinnate and light green but as they are unfurling in the spring they are often flushed with pinkish bronze. Fronds may attain up to 90cm (3ft) in length and they quickly die down once frosts start in the autumn. A native of North America and eastern Asia, this fern is the ideal choice for shrub borders, the fernery, woodland gardens, and the side of a pool where it could be combined with astilbes and moisture-loving primulas, provided there is sufficient shade.

ONOCLEA AT A GLANCE

A tallish pale green herbaceous fern for borders and poolside. Hardy to –15°C (5°F).

		COMPANION PLANTS
JAN	/	Aruncus
FEB	/	Astilbe
MAR	planting	*Hyacinthoides non-scripta*
APR	planting	Magnolia
MAY	foliage	Meconopsis
JUN	foliage	Primula
JULY	foliage	Rhododendron
AUG	foliage	
SEP	/	
OCT	/	
NOV	/	
DEC	/	

CONDITIONS

Aspect The ideal conditions are light dappled shade. This fern also needs shelter from cold winds.

Site Ideally the soil should be acid or neutral. It must also be moisture retentive yet well drained and rich in humus.

GROWING METHOD

Propagation Divide established plants in early to mid-spring. Replant the divisions 60–90cm apart. Can also be propagated from spores and may increase naturally by this method in optimum conditions.

Watering Make sure the plants are watered well and regularly during dry weather.

Feeding Apply an organic slow-release fertilizer in the spring just as growth is under way.

Problems Free from pests and diseases.

FOLIAGE DISPLAY

Season This fern is at its best in spring when the new fronds have emerged, but they last in good condition all summer.

GENERAL CARE

Requirements Cut off dead fronds, close to the crown, in spring before new ones appear. Mulch the plants with organic matter.

OSMUNDA REGALIS
Royal fern

THE GREEN STERILE FRONDS *and rust-brown fertile fronds of* Osmunda regalis *appear almost like two different plants.*

THE FERTILE FRONDS *of* O. regalis *form in a tight bunch in the centre of the plant. They make this fern highly distinctive.*

FEATURES

Sun

The Royal fern is also misleadingly called the 'flowering fern' on account of the 1.8m (6ft) fertile fronds produced in summer that contain rust-coloured spore cases, somewhat resembling a branching flower head. It is a very distinctive waterside fern with upright, wide lance-shaped or triangular, pinnate light green fronds at least 90cm (3ft) long. It is also attractive in autumn when the fronds turn golden brown. With age the royal fern forms large dense clumps with a very fibrous crown. The ideal spot for it is at the side of a pool, otherwise find a really moist spot in a border.

OSMUNDA AT A GLANCE

A distinctive fern for the poolside that has dual seasons of interest. Hardy to −15°C (5°F).

JAN	/	
FEB	/	
MAR	planting 🌱	
APR	planting 🌱	
MAY	foliage 🌿	
JUN	foliage 🌿	
JULY	foliage 🌿	
AUG	foliage 🌿	
SEP	foliage 🌿	
OCT	foliage 🌿	
NOV	/	
DEC	/	

RECOMMENDED VARIETIES
Osmunda regalis 'Cristata'
O. r. 'Purpurascens'
O. r. 'Undulata'

CONDITIONS

Aspect This is one of the few ferns that will grow in full sun, provided the soil is wet or very moist. It will also be happy in dappled shade cast by deciduous trees.

Site Ideally the soil should be acid or neutral. It must also be moisture-retentive, wetter than for most other ferns, and rich in humus.

GROWING METHOD

Propagation Lift and divide established clumps in early to mid-spring. Can also be propagated from spores. These must be sown as soon as they have been collected.

Watering Feeding In dry weather make sure the soil remains wet. This fern likes a fertile soil so apply an organic slow-release fertilizer in the spring just as growth is starting.

Problems Not affected by pests and diseases.

FOLIAGE DISPLAY

Season The royal fern looks good in spring and summer, and also in autumn when the fronds turn golden brown as they die.

GENERAL CARE

Requirements Cut down the dead fronds in spring just before new ones start to unfurl.

POLYPODIUM VULGARE
Common polypody

A USEFUL, HARDY FERN, Polypodium vulgare enjoys well-drained soils and flourishes on rock gardens.

THE DEEPLY CUT LEAFLETS of P. vulgare *make it an interesting contrast to broader- and darker-leaved garden plants.*

FEATURES

Partial shade

The fronds of this dwarf fern are very distinctive. About 38cm (15in) in length, they are sword-like in shape, pinnate, deep green and have a leathery texture. This drought tolerant and hardy fern grows about 30cm (12in) high and has an indefinite spread. The Common polypody is widely distributed in the wild and is found in Europe, Africa and eastern Asia. In the garden it is suitable for growing on a rock garden, and also makes good all-year-round ground cover in a shrub border or on a bank. It is best planted quite densely for ground cover, not more than 45cm (18in) apart each way. The Common polypody is sometimes epiphytic in habit.

POLYPODIUM AT A GLANCE

A dwarf evergreen fern with distinctive, very deeply lobed fronds. Makes good ground cover. Hardy to –15°C (5°F).

JAN	foliage 🌿	RECOMMENDED VARIETIES
FEB	foliage 🌿	*Polypodium vulgare*
MAR	planting ✎	'Bifidocristatum'
APR	planting ✎	P. v. 'Bifidograndiceps'
MAY	foliage 🌿	P. v. 'Bifidomultifidum'
JUN	foliage 🌿	P. v. 'Cornubiense
JULY	foliage 🌿	Grandiceps'
AUG	foliage 🌿	
SEP	foliage 🌿	
OCT	foliage 🌿	
NOV	foliage 🌿	
DEC	foliage 🌿	

CONDITIONS

Aspect It will be happy in dappled shade or full sun but appreciates shelter from cold drying winds that can 'scorch' the fronds.

Site Best grown in well-drained, gritty, reasonably fertile soil rich in humus.

GROWING METHOD

Propagation Division in early to mid-spring is the usual method. Replant divisions 45cm (18in) apart. Can be raised from spores but this method is more of a challenge.

Watering Keep well watered in dry weather, but the common polypody takes drier conditions than most other ferns.

Feeding Apply an organic slow-release fertilizer in spring just as growth is starting.

Problems Not troubled by pests and diseases.

FOLIAGE DISPLAY

Season Foliage is at its best in spring and summer, but being evergreen this fern has year-round interest.

GENERAL CARE

Requirements Remove any dead fronds in spring before the new ones appear. Unlike most other ferns, Common polypody does not need mulching with organic matter. On a rock garden it would have a top dressing of grit or gravel.

POLYSTICHUM
Shield fern

THIS SHIELD FERN has formed a lovely crown of healthy fronds. There is a shield fern suitable for almost every situation.

SHELTER, LIGHT and decaying leaf litter provide ideal conditions for this shuttlecock-shaped shield fern.

FEATURES

Shade

The polystichums are very lacy looking ferns, holding their lance-shaped fronds in shuttlecock formation. They are essential for ferneries, and also look good in shrub borders and woodland gardens. Good companions are spring-flowering shrubs such as rhododendrons and camellias (if you have acid soil) and perennials such as astilbes and candelabra primulas. There are two popular European species. *Polystichum setiferum*, the Soft shield fern, has soft, dark green fronds and grows to a height of 1.2m (4ft) with a spread of 90cm (35in). The Hard shield fern, *P. aculeatum*, with more shiny fronds, reaches a height of 60cm (24in) and spreads to 90cm (35in).

POLYSTICHUM AT A GLANCE

Very lacy-looking, evergreen ferns which look especially attractive with spring-flowering plants. Hardy to −15°C (5°F).

JAN	foliage	RECOMMENDED VARIETIES
FEB	foliage	*Polystichum setiferum*
MAR	planting	Acutilobum Group
APR	planting	*P. s.* Congestum Group
MAY	foliage	*P. s.* Dahlem Group
JUN	foliage	*P. s.* Divisilobum Group
JULY	foliage	*P. s.* 'Herrenhausen'
AUG	foliage	*P. s.* Plumosodivisilobum
SEP	foliage	Group
OCT	foliage	*P. s.* Plumosum Group
NOV	foliage	*P. s.* 'Pulcherrimum Bevis'
DEC	foliage	

CONDITIONS

Aspect These ferns will grow in partial, full or even deep shade.

Site Suitable for any well-drained, reasonably fertile soil containing plenty of humus.

GROWING METHOD

Propagation Division in early to mid-spring. Replant divisions about 90cm (35in) apart. Can also be propagated from bulbils (see page 10). This fern can be raised from spores, but this is a more challenging method.

Watering Water plants regularly during dry weather.

Feeding Just as growth is starting in the spring, apply a slow-release organic fertilizer.

Problems Relatively trouble free, although these ferns can sometimes become infected with a fungal disease.

FOLIAGE DISPLAY

Season These ferns look good all year round but peak seasons are spring and summer.

GENERAL CARE

Requirements Cut off any dead fronds in the spring before the plants start into growth, and at the same time mulch with organic matter. To prevent the crowns from becoming too soggy in very wet winters, support a pane of glass over them, or cover with a cloche.

GROWING PALMS

Palms conjure up images of the tropics, and indeed the vast majority of species are native to tropical or sub-tropical regions of the world. There are a few species that occur in warm and cool climates but they are rare in arid areas and cannot survive in very cold regions.

Palms are grown mainly for their evergreen foliage and are popular garden plants in the warmer parts of the world, but even in areas prone to frosts in winter they can still be used for garden display in summer by growing them in pots or tubs and taking them under cover for the winter. Palms are used extensively for indoor decoration in warm and cold climates.

Palms vary widely in their habits and preferences. Most have tall trunks, either single or several forming a clump. The large compound leaves are popularly known as fronds. These may be fan shaped or very feathery. Palms are long lived and while some reach sufficient maturity to flower within five years or so, others may take about 40 years to start flowering.

LEFT: The pleated fronds of a fan palm radiate outwards and make a dazzling geometric display.

USES IN GARDENS

A palm has a woody trunk that grows with age but it does not start developing that trunk until it has reached a certain size. This accounts for the slow development of some palms. The leaves or fronds arch out from the top of the stem like a crown. Therefore the palm is a very distinctive plant, quite unlike others, capable of providing exotic effects and bringing lushness to the garden. Palms have the advantage that their shape and ultimate size are very predictable, unlike some other trees and shrubs, so there is no excuse for them outgrowing their allotted space. Nevertheless palms have to be used carefully in gardens in cool temperate climates or they will look out of place. There are two ways to use them in these gardens: permanently plant hardy palms to create focal points, or move tender pot-grown palms outside for the summer.

Hardy palms

One of the hardiest palms is *Trachycarpus fortunei*, the Chusan palm, which is frost hardy, taking temperatures down to −5°C (23°F). It is often seen in mild seaside gardens and parks and other favoured areas inland. *Jubaea chilensis*, the Chilean wine palm, is also frost hardy and suitable for growing outside, particularly in mild coastal areas. These two species are also suitable for gardens in towns and cities, which tend to be a few degrees warmer than more open and exposed areas.

These palms can be used as specimen trees, for example in lawns, to create focal points. Or a group of perhaps three can serve the same purpose on a larger scale. They probably look best in formal settings, with good expanses of well-manicured green lawn and formal flower beds containing Large-flowered and Cluster-flowered roses or brightly coloured summer bedding. They also look good beside formal water features such as pools and canals.

Hardy palms are ideal for creating an exotic atmosphere in a courtyard garden. Here they can be used with other 'architectural' or distinctive plants, such as *Fatsia japonica* (Japanese fatsia) with its large evergreen hand-shaped leaves, hostas or plantain lilies, bamboos, the palm-like *Cordyline australis* (New Zealand cabbage palm), ferns of various kinds, and perhaps a hardy grape vine trained to the wall. If the courtyard garden is completely paved, these palms and other plants could be grown in large ornamental tubs and pots. Very fashionable today are blue glazed pots, which make ideal containers for many of these plants.

Hardy palms can also look good in an 'exotic' woodland garden and are sometimes used for this purpose in milder areas. An exotic woodland garden is one on acid or lime-free soil that is planted with rhododendrons, camellias, pieris, magnolias and other choice woodland shrubs and perennials and is a familiar site in many of the large gardens open to the public. This is quite natural for *Trachycarpus fortunei*, for instance, as it is a native of

THIS BUSY, EXOTIC garden in the Scilly Isles takes full advantage of the local climate. The palms in this border are a pleasing jumble of sizes, each one given the space to fulfil its potential but kept in order by the brick wall backdrop.

SUBTROPICAL SUMMER displays are coming back into fashion. Palms can be used to great effect in these exotic plantings.

A FANTASTIC HILLSIDE scene is decked with palms to effect an otherworldly landscape, again created in the Scilly Isles.

forests, particular mountain forests, in sub-tropical regions of Asia. Of course, there is no reason why owners of smaller gardens should not have a woodland garden. All you need is a minimum of one small tree, such as a birch, to create the dappled shade that is loved by these plants. A small group of trees would be even better, if space permits (see also page 7). Hardy palms, if used, should be sited in a more sunny part of the woodland garden, but make sure they are well sheltered from wind.

Tender palms

Tender palms grown in pots and wintered under glass or indoors can be used for summer display out of doors. But place them in shade as sun will scorch the fronds. One way to use them is in formal summer bedding schemes, especially in light shade. The pots can be plunged to their rims in the soil. This prevents root disturbance that would occur if planting them, and also prevents the compost from drying out rapidly. Known as plunge bedding, this method was very popular in Victorian times.

In summer bedding schemes palms can be used as dot plants (specimen plants) in the main carpet of plants, which may be fibrous-rooted begonias, impatiens, fuchsias, and the like. In a small bed, perhaps a single palm could be used in the centre, or in a larger bed maybe a palm could be plunged in each corner with another in the centre.

Plunging is also a technique that can be used to create subtropical summer displays, which are coming back into fashion, having had their heyday in the Victorian period. Again palms can be used, together with other large pot-grown tropical and subtropical plants such as bananas, brugmansias (Angel's trumpets) and cordylines to form the 'framework'. Then smaller subjects, which can be planted normally, are used to fill in, such as cannas (Indian shot), solenostemons (Coleus), fuchsias, and so on. Remember that plunged pots will need regular watering as they will still dry out, albeit not so quickly.

Potted palms can also be brought out for the summer to decorate a patio. Leave them in their pots or tubs and just stand them around, perhaps in combination with tubs of colourful summer bedding plants.

CULTIVATION OUTDOORS

Aspect

The hardy palm *Trachycarpus fortunei* (Chusan palm) can be grown in either full sun or light dappled shade, such as provided by deciduous trees, but *Jubaea chilensis* (Chilean wine palm) needs a position in full sun. Provide shelter from strong winds to avoid the fronds from being torn or scorched. *Trachycarpus fortunei* is more tolerant of winds than other palms but nevertheless it is best to provide it with wind protection. Shelter is best provided by trees and shrubs nearby that filter and slow down the wind. The alternative is to erect, on the windward side, an artificial windbreak made of windbreak netting, but this is unsightly and should only be considered as a temporary measure until trees and shrubs are established.

When standing or plunging potted palms outside for the summer, you will need to take their requirements into account in respect of sun and shade. For information on individual species see the descriptive lists on pages 32–43.

THE VARIOUS SHADES of green created by palm fronds make an interesting texture on their own. However, the careful placing of brightly coloured flowers can also be added to create spectacular highlights. It is important not to overwhelm the garden – single colours are far more effective.

Soil

Palms will thrive in various types of soil and although many will take quite poor conditions, generally the better the soil the better the growth will be.

The ideal soil would be slightly acid to neutral but alkaline conditions are acceptable provided the soil is not a very thin chalky type. Soil should be moisture-retentive but well drained. Avoid sites that become waterlogged in winter as this may result in the death of the palm due to root rot. There should be a good depth of soil so that the palm can root deeply and it should be reasonably fertile.

Before planting, all soils can be improved by digging, to open them up and aerate them, and to provide the opportunity of adding bulky organic matter such as garden compost, very well-rotted manure or composted shredded or chipped bark. Add a generous amount of organic matter to each trench during digging. It provides humus and helps light sandy soils to retain moisture. Organic matter will also open up heavy clay soils, thus helping excess water to quickly drain away.

Planting

Palms are generally bought in containers and come in various sizes, but large ones that are used to create an immediate effect are proportionately more expensive than small specimens, and a deep pocket will be needed to purchase them.

Although container-grown plants can in theory be planted at any time of year, provided the ground is not frozen or very wet, palms are best planted in mid- to late spring when the soil is warming up and drying out. Then they will quickly root into the soil and become established. If they are planted into cold soil they will just sit still and not make new roots, and may then even die, especially if the soil is also wet.

Occasionally large palms may be available rootballed, with the roots enclosed in a ball of soil tightly wrapped in netting or hessian. These are usually plants that have been grown in a nursery field. The same planting time is recommended for rootballed palms in order to get them established quickly.

When preparing the planting hole make sure it is slightly wider than the rootball. The palm should be planted to the same depth as before so make the hole of suitable depth to allow this. The rootball must be moist at the time of planting so if necessary water the plant thoroughly several hours beforehand. When removing the palm from a container aim for as little root disturbance as possible. If planting a rootballed palm, remove the hessian or netting only when the plant is in the hole, to minimize the risk of soil falling away. Return fine soil around the rootball, firming it well with your heels as you proceed. Then water thoroughly to settle the soil around the plant.

Care

During warm dry weather make sure the palms do not dry out. Water them thoroughly whenever the soil starts to become dry. They will also appreciate a mulch of organic matter, such as composted chipped or shredded bark. This will prevent the soil from rapidly drying out during hot dry weather. A layer about 5cm (2in) deep can be applied in spring. The soil should be moist when laying a mulch.

As with trees and shrubs, the best and easiest way to feed palms is to give them an annual application of slow-release organic fertilizer such as blood, fish and bone. This feed is best given in the spring.

For the first few years young palms need to be given additional protection from wind and frost in the winter. A screen made of hessian or windbreak netting can be erected on the windward side. It should be taller than the palm. Alternatively small palms can be surrounded by a cylinder of the same material. To protect roots from severe frosts, young palms can be given a deep mulch of straw for the winter.

Potted palms placed or plunged out of doors for the summer will need to be checked daily for watering – remember that pots can dry out rapidly during hot weather. For watering and feeding of potted palms see Cultivation Indoors, pages 29-31.

Palms do not need pruning, only the removal of dead leaves, which should be cut back to the main stem. This often leaves a pleasant criss-cross pattern on the stem.

CULTIVATION INDOORS

Where to grow

Palms make a delightful addition to an interior and are widely used in homes, offices, hotels, public buildings and the like. However, it should be borne in mind that high light levels are needed plus a humid atmosphere if they are to flourish. The ideal conditions are most easily provided in a conservatory or glasshouse, as long as suitable temperature levels are maintained.

Among the most popular indoor palms are *Howea forsteriana* (Kentia palm), which is slow growing, often an advantage indoors as it does not outgrow its allotted space for years, but it makes good-sized specimens expensive; *Chamaedorea elegans* (Parlour palm) and its relatives; and *Rhapis excelsa* (Miniature fan palm). Many other palms are suitable, too, if you can provide the conditions they require, and have the space, as some grow very large.

Palms generally appreciate a spell outdoors when the weather warms up, so they can be taken outside for the summer and used for garden display (see Uses in Gardens, pages 26–27). Do not move them outside until all danger of frost is over. It should be safe by early summer. And remember to move them back inside before frosts commence in the autumn. The plants should certainly be indoors again by early autumn. Outdoors make sure they are placed in shade, no matter how much light they have been receiving inside, as sun will scorch the fronds.

BACK LIT by the sinking afternoon sun, this row of palms gives the impression of an entire jungle beginning at the foot of this Scilly Isles garden. Palms can be used to make fine, architectural boundary markers, providing a striking backdrop for the rest of the garden.

A WINDING PATH in this Scilly Isles garden takes the observer through a theme park of amazing palm forms and colours. Dense groundcover plants produce a rich carpet from which the striking shapes of the palms can erupt, heightening their dramatic impact on the eye.

Conditions

When growing palms indoors provide bright light but not direct sun that can scorch the foliage. Make sure there are facilities for shading them if necessary during sunny weather. It is essential that a conservatory or glasshouse is fitted with shading blinds, to protect not only palms but also other plants from direct sun. Choose palms suited to the temperatures that you can provide – there are species suitable for cool and warm conditions.

Palms detest dry air that can cause browning of leaf tips, so you will have to provide them with moderate to high humidity according to species. In a conservatory or glasshouse a humid atmosphere is easily provided by damping down the floor and benches and by mist spraying the leaves with plain water. This will need to be done daily in warm conditions, less often in cool conditions.

In the house it is more difficult to provide a humid atmosphere. You may be able to mist spray the leaves if you are careful, but a better method is so stand the pots in trays filled with pebbles or gravel. Keep water under the pebbles but not high enough to reach the pot base. This will ensure the plants are surrounded by humid air.

Care

Water palms moderately when they are in growth, which is from late spring to the end of summer. Moderate watering means providing water when the compost is becoming dry on the surface. For the rest of the year, when the plants are resting or making slower growth, water more sparingly, keeping the compost only just moist. If in doubt, push your finger down into the compost to feel how moist or dry it is. If you can feel moisture then the compost is probably damp enough. Water thoroughly each time, to ensure that the entire depth of compost is moistened. Fill the space between the compost surface and the rim of the pot with water.

Feed palms once a month from late spring to late summer with a balanced liquid fertilizer to keep them growing steadily. A proprietary houseplant fertilizer is suitable, but the compost must be moist.

Palms grown inside are prone to attack by several pests. Scale insects, red spider mites and thrips are the main ones to watch out for. Scale insects are scale-like, motionless insects that you may be able to wipe off with soapy water, or you may need to spray with malathion insecticide. Red spider mites are microscopic creatures whose feeding results in fine pale mottling on the leaves. A humid atmosphere keeps them at bay but if they do attack then spray with malathion or pirimiphos-methyl, or under glass use biological control (the predatory mite *Phytoseiulus persimilis*). Banded palm thrips are tiny insects that cause silvery brown discolouration of the foliage. To control them, spray plants with pyrethrum of permethrin.

Before palms outgrow their pots and become pot-bound (pots densely packed with roots) they should be potted on, using a pot two sizes larger. Once in final-size pots or tubs they need to be repotted into the same size container every two years to provide fresh compost. Tease away some of the old compost from around the roots to make room for the new compost. These operations are best carried out in spring. Soil-based potting compost is suitable, especially for large specimens as it holds them

PALMS ARE USED here for a specific function: to act as elegant features to carry the eye across the formal area in the foreground.

more firmly than soilless compost. In the years between repotting, topdress with fresh compost in the spring, first scraping away about 5cm (2in) of the old compost from the surface.

PROPAGATION

Palms can be raised from seeds, but best results are obtained with fresh seeds, sown as soon as ripe. This is impossible for most people, who will buy seeds rather than collect their own. Purchased seed is best soaked in warm water for at least 24 hours then sown immediately. Also file the hard coats of woody seeds in one or two places to allow moisture to penetrate. Sow seeds singly in deep 9cm (3½in) clay pots, using soilless seed compost. Cover with a layer of compost that equals the seed's own diameter. Big seeds like coconuts are usually half buried.

Germinate seeds in a closed propagating case, as high humidity is needed, at 25–28°C (77–82°F) for tropical species, and 13–18°C (55–64°F) for temperate palms. Seeds of some species may germinate in a few days or several months; others may take a couple of years. Protect seedlings and young plants from direct sun.

Palms such as *Rhapis*, *Phoenix* and some *Chamaedorea* species produce offsets that can be used for propagation. Remove offsets in spring by taking the plant from its pot, scraping soil away to expose the base of the offset, then carefully cutting it off. Pot it in a deep clay pot.

TALL PALMS AND SIMILAR PLANTS WITH spiny fronds act as framing devices for this semi-ruined archway. Palms in general work well with architectural elements in a garden, as their upright forms and starbursts of foliage accentuate the curves and straight lines of buildings.

BUTIA CAPITATA

Jelly palm

THE SPECTACULAR Butia capitata is a highly effective feature palm, with its gently arching branches and sprays of spiny grey-green fronds creating a stunning display. This plant is suitable for growth in a container, but indoor specimens are unlikely to achieve these proportions.

FEATURES

Shade

A native of the cooler parts of South America, this plant is popularly known as the Jelly palm because of its edible but rather tough fruits, which can be boiled to make a jelly. The distinctive grey-green arching fronds consisting of numerous leaflets contrast well with many other palms. This species makes a sturdy trunk from 5–6m (18–20ft) in height and the fronds spread to 3–5m (10–15ft). It is a very long-lived palm but slow growing and ideally suited to cultivation in a container. Suitable for a cool conservatory or glasshouse, it also makes a good houseplant.

BUTIA CAPITATA AT A GLANCE

A slow growing half-hardy palm with distinctive grey-green feathery foliage. Provide a minimum temperature of 5–10°C (41–50°F).

JAN	/	DEC	/
FEB	/		
MAR	planting 🖉		
APR	planting 🖉		
	foliage 🍃		
MAY	foliage 🍃		
JUN	flowering ❀		
JULY	flowering ❀	**COMPANION PLANTS**	
AUG	flowering ❀	Because of the distinctive	
SEP	/	colour of its fronds, *Butia*	
OCT	/	*capitata* contrasts well with	
NOV	/	many other palms.	

CONDITIONS

Aspect Although the Jelly palm needs very bright light it should not be subjected to direct sun or the fronds may become scorched. Provide moderate humidity. If placed outdoors ensure it is sheltered from cold winds to prevent frond damage.

Site In containers grow in soil-based potting compost.

GROWING METHOD

Propagation Raise from seeds sown as soon as available and germinate at 25–28°C (77–82°F).

Watering Moderate watering in growing season from late spring to late summer, then for the rest of the year water sparingly.

Feeding Apply a balanced liquid fertilizer monthly during the growing season from late spring to late summer.

Problems Under glass this palm is prone to attacks by red spider mites and scale insects.

FOLIAGE/FLOWERING

Foliage Looks good all the year round but at its best in the growing season – spring and summer.

Flowers Trusses of yellow flowers in summer are followed by purple fruits.

GENERAL CARE

Requirements Remove dead fronds when necessary by cutting them off close to the trunk.

CHAMAEDOREA ELEGANS
Parlour palm

NEAT FOLIAGE and tolerance of low light levels make the parlour palm most useful. This one shows an immature flower stem.

PARLOUR PALMS are ideal for container growing, indoors or out. A handsome terracotta pot shows this one to advantage.

FEATURES

Shade

A native of Mexico and Guatemala, it is called the Parlour palm because of its widespread popularity as a houseplant. Hailing from a jungle environment, they are quite happy in poorly lit rooms. A smallish palm, it produces a clump of slender stems topped with deep green pinnate fronds about 60cm (2ft) in length. Eventually it reaches a height of 2–3m (6–10ft), with a spread 1–2m (3–6ft). The Parlour palm flowers more freely than many other palms, even indoors, but does not usually set fruits when grown as a houseplant and in any case male and female plants would be needed. A long-lived palm, it is ideal for growing in containers and is a suitable subject for a warm conservatory or glasshouse.

CHAMAEDOREA AT A GLANCE

A smallish palm producing clumps of thin stems topped with rich green feathery fronds. Provide a minimum temperature of 16°C (61°F).

JAN	/	DEC	/
FEB	/		
MAR	planting 🌱		
APR	planting 🌱		
	flowering ❀		
MAY	flowering ❀		
JUN	flowering ❀		
JULY	flowering ❀		
AUG	flowering ❀	RECOMMENDED VARIETIES
SEP	flowering ❀	The variety 'Bella' is more
OCT	/	compact in habit and flowers
NOV	/	more freely than the species.

CONDITIONS

Aspect   Grow the Parlour palm in bright light but do not subject it to direct sun that may scorch the foliage. Provide high humidity. Outdoors avoid windy situations that may result in damage to the fronds.

Site   In containers grow this palm in soilless potting compost.

GROWING METHOD

Propagation   Sow seeds as soon as available and germinate at a minimum temperature of 25°C (77°F).

Watering   Plenty of water in growing season from late spring to late summer, then for the rest of the year water sparingly.

Feeding   Apply a balanced liquid fertilizer monthly during the growing season from late spring to late summer.

Problems   Under glass the Parlour palm is liable to be attacked by scale insects, red spider mites and thrips.

FOLIAGE/FLOWERING

Foliage   Being evergreen the foliage looks good all the year round. At its best in spring and summer.

Flowers   Yellow flowers are produced from spring to autumn and are followed by tiny black fruits.

GENERAL CARE

Requirements   Remove dead fronds when necessary by cutting them off close to the trunk.

CHAMAEROPS HUMILIS
Dwarf fan palm

THE EXPLOSIVE DISPLAY of Chamaerops humilis *fronds, reminiscent of a fireworks display, makes it a useful feature plant.*

C. HUMILIS *FRONDS radiate outwards from the stem. These serve to direct much-needed water to the base of the plant.*

FEATURES

Shade

A native of the Mediterranean region, this is a moderate sized, very bushy, suckering palm with somewhat variable, fan-shaped, pinnate, grey-green or blue-green leaves, up to 1m (39in) in length. These leaves have a very feathery appearance and are highly attractive. The Dwarf fan palm eventually reaches a height of 2–3m (6–10ft), with a spread of 1–2m (3–6ft). It has a moderate rate of growth (it is fully grown after 10 years) and is long lived, making it ideal for growing in containers. This palm rarely grows a full trunk – except in perfect conditions. Suitable for a cool conservatory or greenhouse, it is ideal, too, for growing as a houseplant and it fares especially well outside in the summer.

CHAMAEROPS AT A GLANCE

A bushy suckering palm with fan-shaped, very feathery leaves. Half-hardy, it can take temperatures down to 0°C (32°F).

JAN	/	DEC /
FEB	/	
MAR	planting ✀	
APR	planting ✀	COMPANION PLANTS
	flowering ✿	Looks good with other cool-growing palms and is an
MAY	flowering ✿	ideal subject for combining
JUN	flowering ✿	with brightly coloured
JULY	flowering ✿	summer bedding plants
AUG	flowering ✿	outdoors. Under glass could
SEP	/	combine with
OCT	/	bougainvilleas.
NOV	/	

CONDITIONS

Aspect   Grow the Dwarf fan palm in bright light but do not subject it to direct sun that may scorch the foliage. Provide moderate humidity. Outdoors place in a sheltered position.

Site   In containers grow this palm in soil-based potting compost.

GROWING METHOD

Propagation   Sow seeds as soon as available and germinate them in a minimum temperature of 22°C (72°F). Remove rooted suckers in spring and pot up individually.

Watering   Moderate watering in growing season from late spring to late summer, then for the rest of the year water sparingly.

Feeding   Apply a balanced liquid fertilizer monthly during the growing season from late spring to late summer.

Problems   Under glass this palm may be attacked by red spider mites.

FOLIAGE/FLOWERING

Foliage   This evergreen palm looks good all year round but is especially useful for summer displays.

Flowers   Yellow flowers are produced in spring and summer followed by brown to yellow fruits.

GENERAL CARE

Requirements   Remove dead fronds when necessary by cutting them off close to the trunk.

HOWEA FORSTERIANA
Kentia palm, Thatch leaf palm

THE SLOW GROWTH of Howea forsteriana *makes it a suitable candidate for indoor cultivation. It makes an elegant feature.*

THE FINE LINES running along the length of H. forsteriana's *leaves contribute to the general appearance of this graceful palm.*

FEATURES

Shade

A native of Australia – Lord Howe Island – this is a particularly graceful palm with feathery, gently arching leaves. The slender trunk supports pinnate mid- to deep green leaves that are carried on long stalks and reach 2–3m (6–10ft) in length. This palm will eventually attain a height of up to 18m (60ft), with a spread of 6m (20ft). However, it is fairly slow growing and is therefore good for a container. Potting on or repotting is needed only infrequently. It is suited to a warm greenhouse or conservatory and small specimens are suitable for use as houseplants.

HOWEA AT A GLANCE

A very slender stem supports almost horizontal feathery leaves. Provide a minimum temperature of 15°C (59°F).

JAN	/	DEC	/
FEB	/		
MAR	planting 🖑		
APR	planting 🖑		
	foliage 🌱	COMPANION PLANTS
MAY	foliage 🌱	Under glass it associates well
JUN	flowering ❀	with other palms requiring
JULY	flowering ❀	the same conditions. Also
AUG	flowering ❀	try combining this palm
SEP	/	with tropical foliage plants
OCT	/	such as philodendrons and
NOV	/	*Monstera deliciosa.*

CONDITIONS

Aspect   Provide bright light, but direct sun may scorch the foliage. Provide moderate humidity. Outdoors place in a sheltered position.
Site   In containers grow in soil-based potting compost with leafmould and shredded bark.

GROWING METHOD

Propagation   Sow seeds as soon as available and germinate them at a temperature of 26°C (79°F).
Watering   Moderate watering in growing season from late spring to late summer, for the rest of the year water sparingly.
Feeding   Apply a balanced liquid fertilizer monthly during the growing season.
Problems   Under glass may be attacked by red spider mites and scale insects.

FOLIAGE/FLOWERING

Foliage   This evergreen palm looks good all year but is especially attractive in spring and summer.
Flowers   Clusters of star-shaped flowers are produced in summer, the females green, the males light brown, followed by orange-red fruits.

GENERAL CARE

Requirements   Remove dead fronds when necessary by cutting them off close to the trunk.

JUBAEA CHILENSIS
Chilean wine palm

THE SPACING BETWEEN *the fine leaves of* Jubaea chilensis *give this palm its overall feathery appearance.*

ALTHOUGH SMALL *in its younger years and suitable for indoor settings, J. chilensis eventually grows into a mighty palm.*

FEATURES

Sun

A native of the warm temperate coastal regions of Chile, the Wine palm is a truly massive tree that dominates the landscape. It eventually forms a huge, fat grey trunk topped with a crown of light to deep green pinnate fronds that can grow to 5m (15ft) in length. The trunk contains a lot of sugar, which the Chileans use to make an alcoholic beverage – thus the name. Mature height up to 25m (80ft) with a spread of 9m (28ft). It is slow growing when young but when a trunk has formed it develops more rapidly. When young this is an attractive feathery palm that makes a good houseplant and is ideal too for the cool glasshouse or conservatory. Place it outside for the summer. In favoured areas it can be grown permanently out of doors.

JUBAEA AT A GLANCE

An attractive feathery palm when young with pale to dark green leaves. Frost hardy, taking a minimum temperature of –5°C (23°F).

JAN	/	COMPANION PLANTS
FEB	/	Outdoors combine with
MAR	planting 🌱	colourful summer bedding
APR	planting 🌱	plants, or plants in a sub-
MAY	foliage 🍃	tropical scheme. Under glass
JUN	flowering ✳	grow with *Strelitzia reginae*
JULY	flowering ✳	(Bird of paradise) or *Musa*
AUG	flowering ✳	(banana) species.
SEP	/	
OCT	/	
NOV	/	
DEC	/	

CONDITIONS

Aspect Outdoors grow in a sheltered position in full sun. Indoors provide bright light but do not subject it to direct sun that may scorch the foliage. Provide low to moderate humidity.

Site Outdoors grow in well-drained but moisture-retentive soil. In containers grow in soil-based potting compost.

GROWING METHOD

Propagation Sow seeds as soon as available and germinate them at a temperature of 25°C (77°F). Very slow to germinate.

Watering In containers, moderate watering in growing season from late spring to late summer, then for the rest of the year water sparingly.

Feeding In containers apply a balanced liquid fertilizer monthly during the growing season from late spring to late summer.

Problems Under glass may be attacked by scale insects and red spider mites.

FOLIAGE/FLOWERING

Foliage Being evergreen this palm looks good all year round but is especially attractive in spring and summer.

Flowers Long trusses of small purple and yellow flowers in summer followed by yellow fruits.

GENERAL CARE

Requirements Remove dead fronds when necessary by cutting them off close to the trunk.

LIVISTONA CHINENSIS
Chinese fan palm

THE MODERATE-SIZED Livistona chinensis *(Chinese fan palm) has long stems before the eruption of leaves at the top of the plant.*

A BEAUTIFUL PEACOCK'S tail of leaves makes L. chinensis *a striking houseplant or conservatory specimen.*

FEATURES

Shade

The Chinese fan palm is a native of Japan and Taiwan. Of moderate size when mature, the trunk has a distinctive swollen base. The pinnate, shiny, dark green leaves grow up to 1.8m (6ft) in length and are carried on spiny stalks. The eventual height is up to 12m (40ft), with a spread up to 5m (15ft). This palm, suitable as a houseplant when young, is also recommended for a cool glasshouse or conservatory and is happy to be placed out of doors for the summer. It can be grown in a container for many years.

LIVISTONA AT A GLANCE

The trunk has a distinctive swollen base and supports glossy, dark green leaves. Provide a minimum temperature of 3–5°C (37–41°F).

JAN	/	COMPANION PLANTS
FEB	/	Under glass grow with other
MAR	planting 🌱	palms such as *Jubaea chilensis*
APR	planting 🌱	and with other bold foliage
MAY	foliage 🍃	plants such as *Musa* species
JUN	flowering ❀	(banana), and *Citrus* species.
JULY	flowering ❀	Outdoors combine with
AUG	flowering ❀	colourful summer bedding
SEP	/	plants or include in a
OCT	/	subtropical scheme.
NOV	/	
DEC	/	

CONDITIONS

Aspect	Provide bright light but do not subject it to direct sun. Provide moderate humidity. Outdoors place in a sheltered position.
Site	In containers grow this palm in soil-based potting compost.

GROWING METHOD

Propagation	Sow seeds as soon as available and germinate them at a temperature of 23°C (73°F).
Watering	Water well in growing season from late spring to late summer, then for the rest of the year water sparingly.
Feeding	Apply a balanced liquid fertilizer monthly during the growing season.
Problems	Under glass may be attacked by scale insects and red spider mites.

FOLIAGE/FLOWERING

Foliage	This palm looks good all year round but is especially attractive in spring and summer.
Flowers	Trusses of cream-coloured flowers are produced in summer followed by greyish or bluish fruits.

GENERAL CARE

Requirements	Remove dead fronds when necessary by cutting them off close to the trunk.

PHOENIX CANARIENSIS
Canary Island date palm

CLASSIC PALM FRONDS, as produced by Phoenix canariensis. They are particularly pleasing when they sway in light breezes.

RISING MAJESTICALLY above the lower shrubs, P. canariensis stocky trunk finishes in a triumphant display of arching fronds.

FEATURES

Shade

This well-known and widely grown palm is a native of the Canary Islands. Of medium size, it eventually forms a fat heavy trunk. Wide arching fronds, which are very spiny at the base, grow up to 6m (20ft) in length on mature plants, and carry many bright or deep green leaflets. The mature height is up to 15m (50ft) with a spread of 12m (40ft). As a young specimen this palm makes an ideal houseplant and it can also be recommended for an intermediate to warm conservatory or glasshouse. Place it out of doors for the summer. This palm will produce flowers and fruits in warm climates.

PHOENIX AT A GLANCE

The bright or deep green leaves, consisting of many leaflets, have spiny bases. Provide a minimum temperature of 10–16°C (50–61°F).

		COMPANION PLANTS
JAN	/	Under glass grow with other
FEB	/	palms such as *Howea*
MAR	planting 🌱	*forsteriana*, and with other
APR	planting 🌱	foliage plants like *Monstera*
MAY	foliage 🍃	*deliciosa*. Outdoors combine
JUN	flowering ✺	with brightly coloured
JULY	flowering ✺	summer bedding or
AUG	flowering ✺	subtropical plants.
SEP	/	
OCT	/	
NOV	/	
DEC	/	

CONDITIONS

Aspect Provide bright light but do not subject it to direct sun. Provide moderate humidity. Outdoors place in a sheltered position.

Site In containers grow this palm in soil-based potting compost.

GROWING METHOD

Propagation Sow seeds as soon as available and germinate them at a temperature of 19–24°C (66–75°F).

Watering Water freely in growing season from late spring to late summer, then for the rest of the year water sparingly.

Feeding Apply a balanced liquid fertilizer monthly during the growing season from late spring to late summer.

Problems Under glass may be attacked by red spider mites and scale insects.

FOLIAGE/FLOWERING

Foliage Being evergreen this palm looks good all year round but is especially attractive during the spring and summer.

Flowers In summer trusses of yellow or cream flowers are produced, followed by yellow fruits.

GENERAL CARE

Requirements Remove dead fronds when necessary by cutting them off close to the trunk.

PHOENIX ROEBELENII
Pygmy date palm

THE DELICATE LEAVES of Phoenix roebelenii sprout from equally delicate stems, creating a subtle and elegant palm that can be grown indoors, and outdoors in warm areas. The plant's white flowers are rarely seen in Britain, as it needs warmer conditions for them to set seed.

FEATURES

Shade

A native of Laos in south-east Asia, this is a small, slender, elegant-looking palm of feathery appearance that may be multi- or single stemmed. The leaves, which grow up to 1.2m (4ft) in length, have many shiny dark green leaflets which are somewhat spiky, so be careful where you place it. The eventual height is at least 1.8m (6ft) with a spread of 2.5m (8ft). Widely grown as an indoor plant, it can also be recommended for an intermediate to warm conservatory or glasshouse. It will be happy out of doors for the summer.

PHOENIX AT A GLANCE

An elegant slender palm with long, feathery, dark green shiny leaves. Provide a minimum temperature of 10–16°C (50–61°F).

JAN	/	COMPANION PLANTS
FEB	/	Under glass grow with other
MAR	planting 🌱	palms such as *Howea*
APR	planting 🌱	*forsteriana*, and with other
MAY	foliage 🍃	foliage plants like *Monstera*
JUN	flowering ❀	*deliciosa*. Outdoors combine
JULY	flowering ❀	with brightly coloured
AUG	flowering ❀	summer bedding or
SEP	/	subtropical plants.
OCT	/	
NOV	/	
DEC	/	

CONDITIONS

Aspect	Provide bright light but do not subject it to direct sun. Provide moderate humidity. Outdoors place in a sheltered position.
Site	In containers grow this palm in soil-based potting compost.

GROWING METHOD

Propagation	Sow seeds as soon as available and germinate them at a temperature of 19–24°C (66–75°F). If produced, remove and pot up rooted offsets.
Watering	Water freely in growing season from late spring to late summer, then water sparingly.
Feeding	Balanced liquid fertilizer monthly during the growing period.
Problems	Under glass may be attacked by red spider mites and scale insects.

FOLIAGE/FLOWERING

Foliage	Looks good all year round but is especially attractive in spring and summer.
Flowers	Cream flowers in summer, followed, if male and female plants are grown, by black fruits.

GENERAL CARE

Requirements	Remove dead fronds when necessary by cutting them off close to the trunk.

RHAPIS EXCELSA
Miniature fan palm

THIS INDOOR Rhapis excelsa, *with its dense foliage of widely spaced leaves, adds a lush air to this trellised corner of a conservatory.*

AN EIGHT-LEAVED R. excelsa *frond with distinctive veins running along the length, creating interesting light and dark patterns.*

FEATURES

Shade

A native of southern China, this small palm forms clumps of thin, almost bamboo-like stems. The fan-shaped leaves have long stalks and are divided virtually to their bases, giving the impression of leaflets. This palm was imported to 17th century Japan and became popular among aristocratic circles. A number of cultivars were bred by the Japanese. The leaves of this versatile and undemanding plant are deep green and glossy and can grow up to 30cm (12in) in length. The eventual height and spread of the plant is 1.5–5m (5–15ft), but it is slow growing. Very suitable as a container plant, it makes a good houseplant and is also recommended for the intermediate conservatory or glasshouse. It will also be happy placed out of doors for the summer.

RHAPIS AT A GLANCE

Forms clumps of thin stems topped with fan-shaped, glossy, dark green leaves. Provide a minimum temperature of 10–13°C (50–55°F).

JAN	/	COMPANION PLANTS
FEB	/	Under glass grow with other
MAR	planting 🌱	palms such as *Phoenix* species
APR	planting 🌱	and with other foliage plants
MAY	foliage 🍃	like *Monstera deliciosa*.
JUN	flowering ❀	Outdoors combine this palm
JULY	flowering ❀	with brightly coloured
AUG	flowering ❀	summer bedding or
SEP	/	subtropical plants.
OCT	/	
NOV	/	
DEC	/	

CONDITIONS

Aspect   Provide bright light but do not subject it to direct sun. Provide moderate humidity. Outdoors place in a sheltered position.

Site   In containers grow this palm in soilless potting compost.

GROWING METHOD

Propagation   Sow seeds as soon as available and germinate them at a temperature of 27°C (81°F). Alternatively remove and pot rooted offsets in spring, or divide an entire clump.

Watering   Water freely in growing season from late spring to late summer, then for the rest of the year water moderately.

Feeding   Apply a balanced liquid fertilizer monthly during the growing season from late spring to late summer.

Problems   Under glass may be attacked by red spider mites.

FOLIAGE/FLOWERING

Foliage   Being evergreen this palm looks good all year round but is especially attractive in spring and summer.

Flowers   Clusters of cream flowers are produced in summer followed by white, waxy fruits if fertilization has taken place.

GENERAL CARE

Requirements   Remove dead fronds when necessary by cutting them off close to the trunk.

SABAL PALMETTO
Blue palmetto, Cabbage palmetto

THE TRUNK of the Sabal palmetto *develops a criss cross pattern as the dead fronds are cut back at consistent lengths.*

THE DEAD FRONDS of this S. palmetto *have been trimmed to allow neat, healthy growth to appear at the top of the plant.*

FEATURES

Shade

A native of southern USA (it is the state tree of both Florida and South Carolina), this large palm has a fat, rough-textured trunk and tends to dominate the landscape in the wild. The feathery, fan-shaped leaves are deep green and deeply divided. They attain a length of 1.8m (6ft) and are carried in a somewhat rounded crown. The mature height of this palm is 30m (100ft), with a spread of up to 7m (22ft). As a young plant it makes a good houseplant and is also recommended for the cool conservatory or glasshouse. It likes to be placed out of doors in a bright spot for the summer.

SABAL PALMETTO AT A GLANCE

The dark green, deeply divided, fan-shaped leaves have a feathery appearance. Provide a minimum temperature of 5–7°C (41–45°F).

JAN	/	COMPANION PLANTS
FEB	/	Looks good with other cool-
MAR	planting 🌱	growing palms and is an
APR	planting 🌱	ideal subject for combining
MAY	foliage ✋	with brightly coloured
JUN	flowering ✿	summer bedding plants
JULY	flowering ✿	outdoors. Under glass could
AUG	flowering ✿	combine with bougainvillea.
SEP	/	
OCT	/	
NOV	/	
DEC	/	

CONDITIONS

Aspect   Provide bright light but do not subject it to direct sun. Provide high humidity in summer. Outdoors place in a sheltered position.

Site   In containers grow this palm in soil-based potting compost.

GROWING METHOD

Propagation   Sow seeds as soon as available and germinate them at a temperature of 19–24°C (66–75°F).

Watering   Moderate watering in growing season from late spring to late summer, then water sparingly.

Feeding   Apply a balanced liquid fertilizer monthly during the growing season from late spring to late summer.

Problems   Under glass may be attacked by scale insects and red spider mites.

FOLIAGE/FLOWERING

Foliage   Being evergreen this palm looks good all year round, but it is especially attractive during the spring and summer.

Flowers   Long trusses of cream flowers are produced in summer, followed by small black fruits.

GENERAL CARE

Requirements   Remove dead fronds when necessary by cutting them off close to the trunk.

TRACHYCARPUS FORTUNEI
Chusan palm

THE FOLIAGE of Trachycarpus fortunei *is arranged in neat layers, with the rather stiff fan fronds standing out from the trunk.*

MATURE EXAMPLES of T. fortunei, *with their characteristic covering of dark fibres, here flank a young one.*

FEATURES

Sun

It is not known for certain where this palm originates from but it is probably a native of Burma and China. It gets its common name from the island of Chusan on the east coast of China, where it grows abundantly. It forms a single fibrous trunk topped with fan-shaped, deeply lobed, deep green fronds, which grow up to 75cm (30in) in length. The eventual height is 20m (70ft), with a spread of 2.4m (8ft). The Chusan palm has a reputation as one of the hardiest of all palms, and survives snowy winters. It is therefore hardy enough to be grown out of doors, but in regions subject to very hard winters grow the plant in a tub in a cool conservatory or glasshouse and place it outside for the summer.

TRACHYCARPUS AT A GLANCE

Forms a tall fibrous trunk topped with fan-shaped deeply divided leaves. A frost-hardy palm taking a minimum temperature of –5°C (23°F).

JAN	/	COMPANION PLANTS
FEB	/	Generally grown as a
MAR	planting 🖐	specimen tree in gardens.
APR	planting 🖐	Looks good with formal
MAY	foliage 🖐	beds of roses as well as
JUN	flowering ❀	brightly coloured summer
JULY	flowering ❀	bedding plants.
AUG	flowering ❀	
SEP	/	
OCT	/	
NOV	/	
DEC	/	

CONDITIONS

Aspect   Outdoors grow in a sheltered position in full sun or light dappled shade. Indoors provide bright light but do not subject it to direct sun. Provide low humidity.

Site   Outdoors grow in deep, well-drained but moisture-retentive soil. In containers grow in soil-based potting compost.

GROWING METHOD

Propagation   Sow seeds as soon as available and germinate them at a temperature of 24°C (75°F).

Watering   In containers, moderate watering in growing season from late spring to late summer, then for the rest of the year water sparingly.

Feeding   In containers apply a balanced liquid fertilizer monthly during the growing season.

Problems   Under glass may be attacked by red spider mites and scale insects.

FOLIAGE/FLOWERING

Foliage   Being evergreen this palm looks good all year round but is especially attractive during the spring and summer months.

Flowers   Dangling clusters of small yellow flowers are produced in summer, followed, on female plants, by blue-black fruits.

GENERAL CARE

Requirements   Remove dead fronds when necessary by cutting them off close to the trunk.

WASHINGTONIA
Cotton palm

WASHINGTONIA (COTTON PALMS) *are named for their fine, curled cotton-like threads. These palms are most imposing in maturity.*

THE SHAPELY FRONDS *of this young* Washingtonia *are shown to advantage against this white-painted brick wall.*

FEATURES

Shade

The two species of *Washingtonia* are native to the south-western USA and northern Mexico. They form a single trunk topped with large, fan-shaped, deeply lobed fronds. *Washingtonia filifera* (Desert fan palm, Northern washingtonia), has 2–3m- (6–10ft-) long grey-green leaves with cotton-like threads and an eventual height of 15–20m (50–70ft), with a spread up to 6m (20ft). *W. robusta* (Thread palm, Southern washingtonia) has a tapered trunk topped with 1m- (3ft)- long bright green fronds. Its eventual height is 25m (80ft), and its spread reaches 5m (15ft). Young specimens make good houseplants, or grow them in an intermediate glasshouse or conservatory. Place outside for the summer.

WASHINGTONIA AT A GLANCE

Single-stemmed palms noted for their large fan-shaped, deeply lobed leaves. Provide a minimum temperature of 7–10°C (45–50°F).

JAN	/	COMPANION PLANTS
FEB	/	Good specimen plants for
MAR	planting 🌱	use with summer bedding.
APR	planting 🌱	Under glass grow with
MAY	foliage 🍃	bougainvilleas and
JUN	flowering ❀	*Citrus* species.
JULY	flowering ❀	
AUG	flowering ❀	
SEP	/	
OCT	/	
NOV	/	
DEC	/	

CONDITIONS

Aspect   Provide bright light but do not subject to direct sun. Provide moderate humidity. Outdoors place in a sheltered position.

Site   In containers grow in soil-based potting compost with some leafmould and coarse sand added to the mixture.

GROWING METHOD

Propagation   Sow seeds as soon as available and germinate them at a temperature of 24°C (75°F).

Watering   Moderate watering in growing season from late spring to late summer, then for the rest of the year water sparingly. In winter, keep the soil almost dry.

Feeding   Apply a balanced liquid fertilizer monthly during the growing season.

Problems   Under glass may be attacked by scale insects and red spider mites.

FOLIAGE/FLOWERING

Foliage   Being evergreen these palms look good all year round but are especially attractive in spring and summer.

Flowers   Long arching trusses of cream-white flowers are produced in summer, followed by purple or brown fruits.

GENERAL CARE

Requirements   Remove dead fronds when necessary by cutting them off close to the trunk.

GROWING CLIMBERS

Climbers are among the most useful of garden plants. They provide colour and interest on a higher level without taking up much space near the ground. They are very versatile and can be used in many ways, primarily for covering fences, walls and outbuildings. They can be grown up trellis screens in the garden, and when trained over pergolas will provide shade for a patio or terrace. Suitable climbers can be trained up trees and over large shrubs, and some can be used as groundcover. They can also be grown on free-standing supports in borders.

Climbers can also be used as focal points in a garden by training them over an ornamental arch, say at the end of a pathway. Although few people think of them when planning balcony gardens, they are ideal for this purpose as they take up little horizontal space while decorating an otherwise blank wall.

LEFT: This glorious display of wisteria is at its peak, and it perfectly complements the iron lacework on this long verandah.

WISTERIA SINENSIS *and a white climbing rose have been trained to grow up opposing ends of this metallic arch. With a few more years' growth these plants should tangle together delightfully. The shape of the structure will create a pleasant flowering window between two areas of the garden.*

HABITS OF GROWTH

Unlike the other groups of woody plants, the trees and shrubs, climbing plants do not have self-supporting trunks or stems and therefore use various modifications to lift themselves up towards the light. In their natural habitats there may not always be a convenient support for the plant and so it may trail over the ground or over a rock. We can make use of this method of growth in gardens by using some climbers are groundcover, just allowing them to sprawl over the soil surface. It is a good way of quickly covering large areas, especially banks.

Climbers are grouped into four broad groups according to the mechanism they use to climb: tendril climbers, twiners, scramblers, and self-clinging climbers.

Tendril climbers
Tendril climbers have thin, curling tendrils that coil around their supports, whether it's wire, netting, or trellis. Tendrils are modified organs; in the case of climbers they are generally modified leaves. The grape vine, *Vitis vinifera*, is a good example of a tendril climber. Some tendril climbers, such as *Parthenocissus tricuspidata* (Boston ivy) have adhesive suckers or disks on the tips of their tendrils that stick to smooth surfaces such as walls.

Twiners
Twiners are climbing plants that twine their new shoots entirely around a support. *Wisteria*, which is among our best-loved climbers, is a twiner, and a vigorous one at that. This group of climbers will twine either clockwise or anticlockwise according to species.

Scramblers
Scramblers often climb and support themselves by means of thorns that usually curve downwards, acting as hooks. Climber and Rambler roses come in this group, as do the brambles or *Rubus* species, such as *Rubus henryi* var. *bambusarum*. Scramblers attach themselves to other plants or supports to pull themselves up. Some scrambling plants

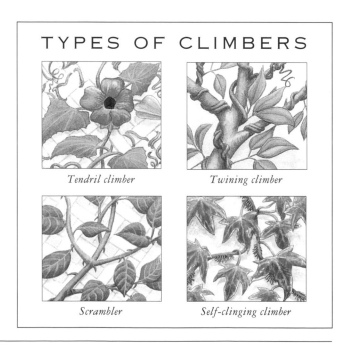

TYPES OF CLIMBERS

Tendril climber

Twining climber

Scrambler

Self-clinging climber

are described as lax, having very long thin thornless stems, an example being *Jasminum nudiflorum* (Winter jasmine). In the wild these just sprawl over other plants or rocks but when grown in gardens they need to have their stems tied in to supports to help them climb.

Self-clinging climbers

Self-clinging climbers are not as common as the other kinds. They produce short roots from their stems, known as aerial roots, that attach themselves firmly to supports. Self-clinging climbers are capable of attaching to completely flat, relatively smooth surfaces such as walls. In the wild they would attach themselves to tree trunks or rock faces. These adventitious roots make their way into any tiny crack or rough patch in the surface of the support. The best-known examples of self-clinging climbers are *Hedera* species (Ivy), *Hydrangea anomala* subsp. *petiolaris* (Climbing hydrangea) and *Schizophragma hydrangeoides*, a relation of the hydrangea.

Matching climbers to supports

Now that we know the methods that climbers use to climb and to support themselves, we can choose suitable plants for the existing supports. On the other hand, if you want to grow a particular climber, you could provide a custom-made support if necessary. Climbers vary tremendously in height and this is an important consideration when choosing plants for the garden.

Some are capable of reaching to the tops of the tallest walls or trees, while others are much less vigorous and will not grow any taller than an ordinary garden fence.

Flamboyant flowers

Apart from their methods of supporting themselves, climbers are diverse in other respects, too. Many are noted for their colourful flower displays. Many hardy climbers have quite flamboyant flowers and are capable of providing an exotic effect in gardens. *Wisteria* is a good example, with its long trusses of pea-flowers, but there are many others such as *Abutilon megapotamicum* (Flowering maple) with red and yellow bells, *Campsis radicans* (Common trumpet creeper) with large orange trumpet-shaped flowers, *Clianthus puniceus* (Glory pea, Lobster claw) with bright red claw-like flowers, *Fremontodendron californicum* with large saucer-shaped yellow flowers, and *Passiflora caerulea* (Blue passion flower), which looks as though it should be grown under glass but which is in fact hardy enough to survive outdoors in many areas.

For sheer quantity of flowers over a long period in summer there is nothing to beat the Climbing and Rambler roses. Some have only one flush of flowers in summer, but if you choose the right cultivars you will get several flushes throughout summer.

Many roses have fragrant flowers, and this is a characteristic of numerous other climbers. For many people the first choice for fragrance, apart from roses,

THIS FINE Clematis 'Etoile Violette' has large, violet flowers with contrasting yellow stamens. The Viticella Group of clematis of which this is one, contains a host of vigorous, free-flowering varieties. These clematis bloom from the midsummer to late autumn.

is honeysuckle such as *Lonicera caprifolium* (Italian honeysuckle), *L. japonica* 'Halliana' (Japanese honeysuckle), and *L. periclymenum* cultivars (Common honeysuckle, Woodbine). Some jasmines also have highly fragrant blooms, especially *Jasminum beesianum, J. humile* 'Revolutum' and, the most fragrant of all, *J. officinale* (Common jasmine). Not related to jasmine, but still with very fragrant flowers, is *Trachelospermum jasminoides* (Star jasmine). And don't forget the reliable *Wisteria* when it comes to fragrance, particularly *W. floribunda* and *W. sinensis* and their various cultivars.

Attractive foliage

Climbers may be deciduous, in other words they lose their leaves in the autumn, or evergreen – retaining their leaves all the year round. The latter are particularly valuable where an object such as a wall needs to be covered all the time. Many climbers are, in fact, grown for their attractive foliage, some of which can be quite exotic-looking, especially the large leaves of the deciduous *Actinidia kolomikta*, which are dark green, pink and white. The evergreen *Euonymus fortunei* cultivars are often brightly variegated and make a splash of colour in a shady situation. The same is true of ivies, both the small-leaved *Hedera helix* cultivars (Common ivy) and cultivars of the large-leaved kinds such as *H. canariensis* (Canary Island ivy) and *H. colchica* (Persian ivy). All have green-leaved cultivars, too. The related X *Fatshedera lizei* (Tree ivy), has large dark green ivy-like leaves, or variegated in some of the cultivars. *Humulus lupulus* 'Aureus' (Golden hop) is one of the most colourful foliage climbers with its golden-yellow, deciduous leaves.

Several deciduous climbers are grown for their autumn leaf colour. Supreme in this respect are species of *Parthenocissus*. Probably the best known and most widely planted is *P. quinquefolia* (Virginia creeper) whose leaves become brilliant red in autumn. Also good are *P. tricuspidata* (Boston ivy) and *P. henryana* (Chinese Virginia creeper). Another superb climber for autumn leaf colour is *Vitis coignetiae*, an ornamental vine, one of the largest-leaved hardy climbers available, whose foliage becomes bright red before it falls.

USES IN GARDENS

Climbers are a highly versatile group of plants and can be used in many ways in the garden. Do not think only in terms of using them to cover a wall. Be more imaginative and adventurous and try using them as free-standing features in beds and borders, growing them over large shrubs, or even using them as groundcover.

It is important that climbers are matched to their supports, so bear this in mind when choosing plants for your garden. Some climbers are very vigorous and only suitable for covering the largest walls, and would

DESPITE ITS YOUTH, a young honeysuckle plant nevertheless provides a bright show of vibrant red flowers. This species, Lonicera x brownii *'Fuchsioides', is quite hardy and will make a good wall-covering climber. It flowers throughout the summer.*

A TRELLIS makes the perfect support for this Clematis macropetala *'Markham's Pink'. The plant will grow leaving decorative windows.*

THE LINES of this trellis are consumed by a mass of Parthenocissus *leaves. Climbers will help any object to blend into the garden.*

therefore need a lot of pruning to keep them within bounds. On the other hand there are many of more modest stature, suitable for even small gardens.

Walls and fences

It is safe to say that all climbers can be grown on walls. On the walls of the house it is probably best to avoid those that produce aerial roots such as ivies, and tendril climbers with adhesive suckers like *Parthenocissus*, for not only are they vigorous but once attached are very difficult to remove. These would be better for tall boundary walls. Instead, for the average house, go for more manageable climbers such as roses, *Clematis* and jasmines; or wall shrubs such as *Abutilon megapotamicum* (Flowering maple), *Chaenomeles speciosa* (Flowering quince), *Cotoneaster horizontalis* (Fishbone cotoneaster) and *Fremontodendron californicum* (Flannel bush). Wisterias are often grown on house walls but bear in mind that they are tall, vigorous climbers and need a lot of pruning. They are probably better for large houses.

For boundary fences, which are generally about 1.8m (6ft) high maximum, such as close-boarded or panel fences, again use the smaller, more manageable climbers as suggested above. If you have a chain-link fence you could choose from the group known as twiners. These will support themselves by twining their shoots through the mesh. Wisterias are twiners, and although very tall, they can be grown on low fences by training the stems horizontally. *Muehlenbeckia complexa* is another twiner suitable for covering chain-link fencing.

Pergolas, arches and arbours

These are excellent supports for many climbers but not for those that produce aerial roots like ivies, or adhesive suckers such as *Parthenocissus*. Favourites for pergolas are grape vines, *Vitis vinifera*, either fruiting or ornamental kinds, which quickly provide welcome shade over a patio. Climbing roses are also popular, and look especially attractive trained over an arch or arbour. Roses can be grown with *Clematis*, allowing the two to intertwine for some really stunning effects. *Wisteria*, again, is a favourite for larger pergolas, especially as the dense flower trusses hang down inside the structure.

Obelisks for borders

Few people think of growing climbers in beds and borders as free-standing specimens. Yet this is an excellent way to grow the smaller kinds such as Large-flowered climbing roses, *Clematis* (try combining the two), and *Humulus lupulus* 'Aureus' (Golden hop). Obelisks make ideal supports, and are obtainable in steel or wood. Woven hazel or willow obelisks are also available and their rustic appearance makes them ideal for cottage or country gardens. DIY enthusiasts could probably save some money by making their own obelisks out of timber.

Trees and shrubs

Large mature trees make suitable supports for tall vigorous climbers such as *Rosa filipes*, particularly the cultivar 'Kiftsgate'. With its white flowers, this is very effective when grown through a large mature dark green conifer. Ivies, *Parthenocissus*, *Hydrangea anomala* subsp. *petiolaris* (Climbing hydrangea) and other self-clinging climbers are suitable for big deciduous trees. Thin-stemmed, light and airy climbers such as *Clematis viticella* cultivars can be grown through large mature shrubs.

THIS SOLANUM CRISPUM *hangs lush and colourful over a bed of assorted plants. The addition of a climber can lift an entire bed and completes the decorative effect. Plantings should be thought out with the use of climbers in mind – they can revolutionize your entire garden look.*

Ugly outbuildings
To quickly cover and hide ugly outbuildings such as sheds and garages choose a vigorous climber. These include plants such as *Ampelopsis glandulosa* var. *brevipedunculata* 'Elegans', *Campsis radicans* (Common trumpet creeper), *Celastrus orbiculatus* (Staff vine), the extremely vigorous *Fallopia baldschuanica* (Russian vine), *Hedera colchica* (Persian ivy), or *Parthenocissus* species.

Pots and tubs
While most climbers are planted directly in the open ground, some can also be grown in tubs and pots. For example, if you have a pergola built over a paved area such as a patio, or you want to grow a climber on a patio wall, there may be no soil available in which to plant. Large containers filled with soil-based potting compost will make suitable homes for the less-vigorous climbers. The container needs to be a minimum of 30cm (12in) in diameter and depth; 45cm (18in) or larger would be better. A good depth is particularly important as then the compost will not dry out quickly and the climber will be able to root deeply, resulting in better growth.

Less-vigorous climbers are best suited to containers as then they will not quickly outgrow them. Many *Clematis* are ideal, particularly the summer-flowering Large-flowered hybrids and the *C. viticella* cultivars. Other suitable plants you might like to try include *Abutilon megapotamicum* (Flowering maple), *Clianthus puniceus*

(Glory pea, lobster claw), X *Fatshedera lizei* (Tree ivy), hederas (Ivies), *Humulus lupulus* 'Aureus' (Golden hop) and Large-flowered climbing roses (these need a large tub). Very vigorous climbers should not be attempted, although wisterias are sometimes trained as standards (like small trees, with a single stem) in large tubs, and they make unusual features on a patio. *Vitis vinifera* (Grape vines) can be grown in the same way.

Container-grown plants will need extra maintenance in the way of regular watering and feeding through the year, but the results are certainly worthwhile.

Ground cover
Some climbers make excellent groundcover, say among shrubs, under trees, or even for covering a steep bank. *Cotoneaster horizontalis* (Fishbone cotoneaster), although a wall shrub rather than a climber, is often used for this purpose. It has a prostrate, spreading habit of growth when used for ground cover.

Euonymus fortunei cultivars make excellent evergreen groundcover and are particularly good for growing in shady areas of the garden, although the variegated cultivars develop a better colour when exposed to at least some sun. The same applies to ivies. The small-leaved *Hedera helix* cultivars (Common ivy) create a marvellous flowing texture when grown as groundcover, and the large-leaved ones such as *H. colchica* (Persian ivy) create a different but still pleasing effect.

THIS CLIMBING ROSE has managed to extend itself across the entire width of this house, and is enlivening the whole of the front of the house with an amazing abundance of light pink flowers. At this height, dead-heading becomes a major effort – but as this picture shows it is well worth the trouble.

Parthenocissus can be used for covering large areas and is effective when cascading down a bank, especially in autumn when the leaves turn brilliant red, giving the effect of a stream of molten lava.

PROVIDING SUPPORTS

Many climbers, apart from the self-clinging kinds, need a bit of extra help to climb their supports. For example, they will not be able to hold on to a wall or fence, or the pillars of a pergola, without some additional support. And free-standing climbers in beds and borders, for instance, will need some kind of structure to climb.

Walls and fences
The traditional method of supporting climbers on walls and fences is with a system of horizontal wires, to which the stems of the climbers can be tied as they grow. Heavy gauge galvanized or plastic-coated wire is recommended for this purpose. The wires, which can be spaced about 30–45cm (12–18in) apart up the wall or fence, can be stretched tightly between vine eyes, which are like screws but with a ring at the top. Provide one of these at each end of the wire, and if it is a long stretch insert one or two in between to prevent the wire from sagging too much. To achieve really tight wires you may have to use stronger devices such as straining bolts instead of vine eyes.

CLIMBERS FOR GROWING AS GROUND COVER

- *Akebia quinata* (Chocolate vine)
- *Ampelopsis glandulosa* var. *bevipedunculata* 'Elegans'
- *Clematis*, Viticella Group
- *Cotoneaster horizontalis* (Fishbone cotoneaster)
- *Decumaria barbara*
- *Euonymus fortunei*
- *Hedera canariensis* (Canary Island ivy)
- *Hedera colchica* (Persian ivy)
- *Hedera helix* (Common or English ivy)
- *Hydrangea anomala* subsp. *petiolaris* (Climbing hydrangea)
- *Lonicera periclymenum* (Common honeysuckle)
- *Parthenocissus henryana* (Chinese Virginia creeper)
- *Parthenocissus quinquefolia* (Virginia creeper)
- *Parthenocissus tricuspidata* (Boston ivy)
- *Rubus henryi* var. *bambusarum* (Bramble)
- *Schisandra chinensis*
- *Schizophragma hydrangeoides*
- *Trachelospermum jasminoides* (Star jasmine)
- *Vitis coignetiae* (Vine)
- *Vitis vinifera* 'Purpurea' (Grape vine)

Vine eyes hold the wires a short distance away from the wall, and this allows free circulation of air between the wall and the plants. Good air circulation is particularly recommended for house walls to prevent the possible development of dampness. It also lessens the risk of diseases attacking the plants.

The alternative to horizontal wires is to fix trellis panels to walls and fences, to which climbers can be tied. Available in wood, metal or plastic, they can generally be fixed to the wall with rust-proof screws, placing a wooden block between the wall and the panel wherever screws are used, to ensure a space of at least 5cm (2in) for air circulation. Old cotton reels make good 'buffers'.

Wires or trellis panels can also be used on outbuildings to support climbers. A particularly unsightly building can be made more attractive by completely covering the walls with attractive wooden trellis.

Substantial and long-lasting materials are needed to tie in climbers to their supports. The traditional material is tarred string which has a long life. Otherwise use ordinary thick garden string or twine. Small proprietary plastic ties of various kinds are also suitable. Do not use wire, as this will cut into the stems.

Pergolas, arbours and arches

A pergola is one of the most popular supports for climbers. It is a tall garden structure that can take various forms. Basically it consists of a series of pillars. These are generally made of timber, but pillars can be constructed with brick or natural stone, these being more suitable for large gardens as they are bulky structures. The pillars support horizontal beams.

Pergolas can be various shapes but the most popular is to have pillars along each side of a path linked by cross beams, thus creating a covered walk. Also popular is a square or rectangular pergola covering or partially covering a patio or other paved area that is used for outdoor living, the idea here being to create a pleasant shady area in which to sit, relax and enjoy alfresco meals.

It is possible to buy pergola kits. Timber is the most popular material for construction and is available from many DIY superstores and garden centres. Metal pergolas, available from specialist suppliers, are more expensive. DIY enthusiasts may be able to construct their own timber pergola, using smooth, pressure-treated timber or, for a country or cottage garden, rustic poles.

Arches also make good supports for climbers, again available in kit form, timber or metal. They consist of upright pillars with cross pieces at the top and are generally used to form an entrance – again, perhaps, placed over a path. These can be highly effective with a flowering climber draping itself overhead.

An arbour or bower is a traditional support for climbing plants. These are essentially intimate alcoves where one can sit and enjoy a pleasant view of the garden. An arbour is often combined with a pergola, being placed

A FETCHING ARCH over a path, seating area and lavender bed benefits from a climber. Used with architectural elements, climbers act to soften harsh lines and help to make objects such as this arch to merge into the general flow of the garden.

BIRDS LOVE the twisting branches of climbers as sites for their nests. Here a clematis provides decoration and a home.

THIS LARGE-FLOWERED Clematis cultivar has a good hold on a timber post, and provides a column of vibrant colours.

at the end of a path. There are timber or metal versions available, but the DIY enthusiast may be able to construct one from wooden trellis panels.

Most climbing plants will need some help to grow up the timber pillars used for garden structures, as well as brick or stone pergola pillars. Vertical wires can be fixed to pillars, to which the climbers can be tied, again using vine eyes or even ordinary screws which end up looking less conspicuous. Generally there is no problem tying in climbers to metal structures, and no additional support is needed to keep the plants in place.

Free-standing supports

To grow climbers, such as clematis and roses, in a bed or border you will need to provide some kind of support. Very popular are obelisks, specially designed for the purpose. Proprietary ones are available in metal or wood. If you want a more rustic kind, opt for woven willow or hazel designs. Obelisks come in various heights – make sure you choose a suitable height for your subject. For most climbers 1.8m (6ft) would be the minimum. Pot obelisks are also available for patio tubs. Simply tie in climbers to these supports with garden twine.

Alternative supports for climbers in beds and borders are wooden pillars. Stout fencing posts about 2.4m (8ft) long are ideal for the purpose, and should be sunk about 60cm (24in) into the ground. Provide a vertical wire on each side of the post for tying in the climber.

Growing up trees

Climbers other than self-clinging kinds will need additional means of support on large trees until they reach the branches, which will then take over as supports. So to start with insert long bamboo canes into the ground against the trunk of the tree, one for each stem. The young stems can then be tied into these with garden twine. Self-clinging climbers generally need to be provided with just one shorter cane after planting to initially guide the young stem to the trunk.

GROWING CONDITIONS

To ensure optimum growth and flowering from your climbers you must grow them in the right conditions. It is a case of choosing exactly the right spot in your garden for the particular plant, taking into account aspect and soil conditions. Specific conditions are given for each climber in the plant section (see pages 64–109).

Aspect

The majority of climbers grow best in sites with full sun but there are some that tolerate partial shade, in other words, where the sun reaches for part of the day only. Others will take full shade, with no sun at all. Some climbers like the best of both worlds – an example being clematis, which like a cool shaded root run but their heads in the sun. To achieve this, grow them in a sunny spot but ensure their roots are shaded by shallow rooting, low growing or ground-cover plants. Heavy mulching over the root area will achieve the same result.

South- and west-facing walls and fences are usually the sunniest and warmest areas of the garden, while north- and east-facing ones are the coolest and shadiest. Those facing east receive some sun in the morning while northerly aspects receive no sun at all.

Many climbers need shelter from strong winds, not only to prevent their stems being whipped around and damaged (although if tied in properly this should not happen), but also to prevent the foliage being scorched by cold drying winds. Some of the less hardy climbers in particular need a warm, sheltered spot to ensure good growth and flowering. If the garden is not naturally sheltered, wind protection can be provided in various ways, for example by planting large wind-resistant shrubs on the windward side of the garden to filter and slow down the wind. Also large shrubs planted further in the garden to form a screen can have the effect of creating a favourable microclimate for less-hardy plants. Sheltered courtyards are also ideal for the less-hardy climbers.

Soil

There are climbers to suit all types of soil, from heavy clay, through loams, to chalky types and light sandy soils, and from moisture-retentive to dry. The majority of climbers will grow well in any type of soil if it has been well prepared, and in both acid (lime-free) and alkaline (limy) soils. Some, however, prefer limy or chalky soils, such as clematis, while others must have acid conditions,

an example being *Berberidopsis corallina*, although it would survive in neutral soil. Check your soil for acidity or alkalinity (also called its pH) with a simple soil-testing kit, obtainable from many good garden centres.

Many climbers are long-lived plants and respond well to thorough soil preparation and improvement before planting. In particular it is important to ensure that the soil is adequately drained and does not become waterlogged in the winter. Soil is prepared by digging to the depth of the spade blade and at the same time any improvements can be carried out.

Loamy soils are the best, being fertile and well-drained, and need little in the way of improvement. However, even these benefit from the addition of bulky organic matter during digging, adding it to the bottom of each trench and then forking it in. You can use garden compost, well-rotted manure or composted bark. These all break down in the soil and become humus that helps to improve the structure of all soils and also aids in the retention of moisture and nutrients.

Clay soils may be poorly drained. To improve drainage, again incorporate bulky organic matter, but also add copious amounts of horticultural grit or coarse sand if

A POPULAR CLIMBER, Wisteria floribunda *'Multijuga' arranges itself in a pleasantly regular fashion over the rear of this house. Its pendulous blooms of lilac-blue make a striking textural as well as colourful display. These flowers appear in late spring and early summer.*

drainage is poor. These materials open up the soil and improve both drainage and air circulation. Add sand or grit to the bottom of the trenches during digging and also mix it into the top 30cm (12in) of soil.

Adding bulky organic matter to the freely drained chalky and sandy soils, which are inclined to dry out rapidly, will help them to retain moisture during dry periods. Unfortunately the humus thus created does not last long in these soils, but can be replaced by the application of a heavy mulch.

Following the initial preparation of a planting site, leave the ground to settle for a few months before planting. Then just before the plants go in fork a general-purpose fertilizer into the surface.

Planting

As with most plants these days, climbers are bought in pots, whether from a garden centre or from a mail-order nursery. So they can be planted at any time of year because their roots are not disturbed when planting. However, never plant when the soil is cold and wet, or frozen, in the winter as the roots may rot before the plant has a chance to become established. It is not a good idea to plant during drought conditions as then much more water will be needed to get plants established. The ideal time to plant is in the spring, as the soil is warming up and drying out. Then the plants will quickly root into the soil and become established. Some gardeners also favour autumn planting, while the soil is still warm.

To plant a pot-grown climber, make a planting hole slightly wider than the rootball, and of such a depth that after planting the top of the rootball is only just below the soil surface. Return fine soil around the rootball, firming it well with your heels or fist as you proceed.

If initial supports are needed, such as a bamboo cane to guide the stems to the main support, insert this before returning soil around the plant, to avoid pushing it through the roots, which may damage them.

It is the usual practice to set climbers at least 30cm (12in) away from a wall or fence and to guide the stems to the support with bamboo canes angled in towards it. This is because the soil can be very dry immediately in front of a wall or fence, because rain is deflected, so climbers may not establish well in this 'rain shadow'. The same applies when planting against a large tree. After planting, mulch the plants with bulky organic matter.

When planting in pots and tubs, first put a 5cm-(2in-) deep layer of drainage material in the bottom (broken clay flower pots or pebbles), cover this with a layer of chipped bark, then use a good soil-based potting compost to fill the container. Half fill the container, set the plant in the centre, then fill up with more compost.

GENERAL CARE

Having taken care to get your new climbers off to a good start by preparing the soil well and planting them correctly and in the best positions, it is sensible to look after them well for the rest of their lives. They will repay you with healthy growth and prolific flower displays.

Mulching

A modern gardening trend is to permanently mulch the ground between plants in beds, including shrubs, climbers and hardy perennials. This will help to prevent the soil

STAR JASMINE is widely grown for its dark, glossy foliage and heavily scented white flowers. It will soon twine around this post.

from losing moisture rapidly during dry periods and also acts to prevent weeds establishing themselves. It can also give the bed a neater appearance than bare soil.

However, the ground must first be completely free from weeds, particularly perennial kinds, before laying a mulch. Perennial weeds will force their way up through organic mulching materials, so if necessary kill them off first with glyphosate weedkiller. A modern idea is to lay a geotextile sheet mulch, such as bonded fibre fleece or woven polypropylene, around plants to suppress weeds and then cover it with a more decorative, such as an organic, mulching material. Sheet mulches allow air and water to pass through, but do make it quite difficult to apply fertilizer around plants.

Organic mulches are widely used. A particular favourite is chipped bark or wood, used both fresh and composted, and available in various grades and wood to bark ratios. Garden compost and well-rotted manure are also good but not as attractive as bark. These materials are laid about 5cm (2in) deep over the entire bed or border, but not hard up against the stems of plants.

An organic mulch can initially be laid in the spring and then topped up as necessary. The soil must be moist rather than dry before laying a mulch.

Watering

All newly planted climbers, like any other plants, will need regular watering if the soil starts to dry out, until they become established. Until new roots have made their way into the soil plants are very susceptible to water stress. Check new plantings every few days during dry weather in spring, summer and autumn and if the soil feels dry water heavily. When plants are established they usually need watering only during long periods of dry weather, if the soil is drying out.

Apply sufficient water for it to penetrate the soil to at least 15cm (6in). This means about 18 litres per sq/m (4 gal per sq/yd). This equals about 2.5cm (1in) of rain. Use a garden sprinkler or, even better, a permanent seep hose laid among the plants, ideally under a mulch.

Pots and tubs will need checking daily in spring, summer and into autumn for water requirements. Remember they can dry out rapidly in warm weather, especially when plants are well rooted in them. Fill up the space, usually about 2.5cm (1in), between the compost surface and the rim of the pot with water to ensure the entire depth of compost is moistened.

Feeding

Established climbers benefit from an annual application of fertilizer in the spring. Use a general purpose slow-release fertilizer. A good organic one is blood, fish and bone. The soil should be moist, but not sodden, when the fertilizer is applied. If the soil has a mulch over it you will need to scrape this away from the plants before applying fertilizer. Ideally fertilizer should be lightly forked into the soil surface to speed up its absorption.

Climbers in pots and tubs can also be fed once a year in the spring, again using a slow-release fertilizer that will keep them going throughout the growing season.

Tying in

If necessary, the young stems of climbers should be tied in to their supports as they grow. This will prevent them being whipped around by the wind or snagged by passers-by and damaged. It is always easier to train stems when they are young and supple, because as they age they become more woody and therefore difficult to position exactly where you want them. Mature stems are also more prone to snapping. Stems should always be spaced out evenly on the support and tied in with tarred or ordinary garden twine or small plastic ties.

Winter protection

Some climbers and wall shrubs are less hardy than others and could be damaged by hard frosts. If you are tempted to grow any of these and live in a cold part of the country it would be advisable to provide some form of protection during the winter, particularly for the lower parts of the stems to prevent these being killed off. A protective screen about 1.8m (6ft) high can be formed from two sheets of wire netting with a layer of bracken or straw sandwiched in between them. Wire them together then

THIS PRETTY PINK jasmine, Jasminum beesianum, *has found itself a pleasant spot nestled in the corner of a large pergola. It makes a wonderfully bright highlight in what would otherwise have been a rather dull and uninteresting corner. It also provides scent to fragrance the area.*

MAKING FULL USE of each plant's habit of growth, this meeting of white foxgloves from below and white climbing roses from above makes for an upward sweeping movement.

ENJOYING PERFECT health, this clematis shines forth with an abundance of scarlet flowers, enhanced with bright yellow stamens.

form the 'sandwich' into a half cylinder and place it in front of the climber, hard up against the wall or fence. This should provide sufficient protection from hard frosts. If the tops of the stems are killed by frost, cut them back to live tissue in the spring, and they should re-grow.

Pests and diseases
Fortunately most climbers are not troubled much by pests and diseases. Occasionally they may be attacked by aphids or greenfly but these are easily controlled by spraying with an insecticidal soap or pyrethrum. These products will also control any infestations of caterpillars. Powdery mildew may crop up occasionally, particularly on grape vines, creating a white deposit on the leaves and shoot tips. If you notice this on the plant, spray it with a fungicide such as carbendazim.

One or two climbers, however, have more than their fair share of troubles, particularly roses. These may be attacked by the diseases rose black spot (black spots on leaves), rose rust (rust-coloured spots on leaves), and rose powdery mildew. Aphids (greenfly) are also very fond of roses. Wherever possible buy cultivars that are resistant to diseases, particularly black spot. If you have to resort to spraying, opt for a combined rose spray that controls pests and diseases. Very often rose diseases can be prevented by spraying regularly before they appear.

Clematis are prone to a very serious fungal disease known as clematis wilt, which causes shoots and foliage to wilt and die back. If this occurs, cut back affected stems to healthy wood. It may even be necessary to remove stems at ground level or below. If the attack is not too severe, the plant should produce new growth.

PRUNING AND TRAINING

Many climbers do not need regular pruning, only the occasional removal of old and congested growth. This is just as well as pruning these plants is a time-consuming process, much of which may have to be done from ladders or stepladders. However, some climbers do need annual pruning to keep them under control and to ensure good growth and flowering. These need to be grown where they are easily reached and not, for example, up a tall tree or very high wall. Specific pruning requirements and when to prune are given for each climber in the plant section (see pages 64–109). The various techniques for pruning climbers are discussed here.

Basic techniques
You will need a good pair of parrot-bill secateurs for pruning thin stems, for example when you are spur pruning a wisteria. You will also need a pruning saw or heavy-duty loppers (like long-handled secateurs) to tackle thick growth, such as when you are renovating an old climber. Shears are useful for pruning or trimming some climbers, particularly those which produce a mass of thin stems such as hederas (ivies) and loniceras (honeysuckles). It would be too time consuming to prune these stems individually with secateurs so shears are used to considerably speed up the job.

Always use really sharp tools to ensure clean cuts that heal more rapidly than ragged cuts made with blunt implements. The latter may encourage the entry of diseases, resulting in stems dying back.

IVIES ARE among the most frequently seen climbers. Many varieties are vigorous growers and some can be invasive, smothering formal beds. Under close supervision, however, they make superb groundcover (above) as well as excellent climbers, with some species displaying variegated foliage.

Individual pruning cuts, for example when spur pruning, are made directly above a bud on the stem. Always cut to a bud that points in the direction that you want growth to occur. Never cut back to buds that face in towards the wall or other support. Do not leave a length of stem or 'stub' above a bud, as it will only die back and look unsightly and may create an entry point for diseases. If stems have buds arranged alternately, make the cut slightly slanting, in the direction that the bud is pointing, to allow rainwater to run off. If there are pairs of opposite buds, as in clematis for example, make a straight cut just above them.

There is no need to seal pruning cuts, although very large wounds, such as occur when cutting out old, thick wood, could be sealed with proprietary pruning 'paint' to prevent moisture and diseases from entering. If you are pruning plants that are diseased, you should regularly disinfect your tools by wiping the blades with methylated spirit or dipping them in horticultural disinfectant.

It is important to prune climbers at the right time of year. Generally deciduous climbers are pruned in the winter while they are dormant, ideally in late winter, and evergreens in the spring, when they will rapidly produce new shoots to hide the pruning cuts. Some flowering climbers are pruned in spring or summer immediately after the flower display is over.

Initial training
Before planting a new climber, remove any weak, dead or damaged stems. If it has only one or two stems and you want more, cut out the tips to encourage new shoots to be produced from lower down. Some young climbers have only a single stem when purchased, including many clematis. It is best to allow such plants to become established over a complete growing season before cutting back the stem in early spring to encourage more stems to grow. With clematis the stem can be cut back really hard, near to the soil. Other climbers can have their stem reduced by one-third to half its length.

Tie in the stems of all climbers after planting, whatever their habit of growth may be, and keep them tied in as they grow. Self-clinging climbers do not adopt this habit to start with so keep them tied in until they can support themselves.

In the first few years young climbers do not need much pruning but you should concentrate on training the stems to their supports. If the plant is neither branching enough nor making sufficient stems to cover a given area, then cut back the leading shoots to encourage the production of side shoots.

Aim to develop a basic framework of stems that covers the support well. Train the stems as evenly as possible, making sure they are well spaced out, especially on a wall or fence where they can be trained to a fan shape. Bear in mind that stems trained horizontally often flower much better than those trained vertically. The same applies to stems spiralled around the support, such as a post or pillar. Some flowering climbers, such as wisterias, can have all their stems trained horizontally, on a low fence or wall for example, which will encourage prolific flowering. Climbing and Rambler roses also respond especially well to horizontal training.

Stems are trained vertically on pillars and posts, or they can be spiralled around the support to encourage better flowering. When the stems reach the top of structures such as pergolas, arches and arbours they are trained horizontally over the structure.

Regularly cut out any shoots that are growing in towards the wall or growing outwards, or train them in a different direction. Do not allow stems to grow across each other. Any shoots that are not needed for the main framework can be cut back to at least three buds. They may then produce flowers.

Annual spur pruning

Much annual pruning of established climbers to encourage the production of flowers or fruits, and prevent congested growth, takes the form of spur pruning. It is generally deciduous climbers that produce their flowers on shoots produced in the current season, such as climbing roses, that are spur pruned. In late winter side shoots produced from the main framework are cut back to within three to six buds of their base. These spurs develop to produce flowers later in the year.

However, if the climber flowers on shoots produced in the previous year, it should be spur pruned as soon as flowering season is over, an example of this being *Jasminum nudiflorum* (Winter jasmine).

Very vigorous climbers such as wisteria are pruned twice a year, once in summer to reduce the length of the vigorous side shoots, and then in winter when they are reduced further, to within two or three buds of their base.

Trimming

Established climbers that do not need regular pruning, such as hederas (ivies), *Clematis montana* and its cultivars and *Lonicera* (honeysuckle) species and cultivars, produce a heavy mass of growth over a period of time and need cutting back with shears to reduce their bulk. They can be pruned hard back to their support in late winter or early spring, just leaving the main framework of stems which will then produce a fresh crop of new growth. To prevent ivies from becoming bulky they can, alternatively, be trimmed annually in spring.

Thinning and renovating

Established climbers that are not pruned regularly may eventually need to have their main body of growth thinned out. It is not advisable to allow plants to become too congested before pruning, as it will then involve a large amount of work and may end up spoiling the overall appearance of the plant. Thinning will help to prevent the plant from becoming too heavy and congested and allows light and air to reach the centre, which is necessary for continued healthy growth.

The technique involves cutting back some of the older stems to younger shoots lower down which will then replace them. Alternatively old stems may be cut down fairly close to the ground to encourage them to produce

AN OLD WISTERIA in full bloom grows over an arch where the lovely pendulous flowers can be best appreciated.

THE FROTHY flowers of this rose are trained to poke through the trellis. Intertwined ivy is set off beautifully by the stained blue wood.

new shoots from very low down. Always cut out stems in short sections as it makes the job easier. Trying to pull out a long stem from a congested mass of growth is not only difficult but can also damage the plant. In a dense mass of growth it is not always easy trace the entire length of a stem, and you may cut out a young vigorous stem by mistake. To overcome this problem, cut back an old stem, even close to the ground, and then wait a few days for it to wilt so that it can be easily seen.

If a climber has been badly neglected and not pruned for years (perhaps in a garden that you have recently inherited from a previous owner) some drastic action may be called for to rejuvenate it. If the plant is a species that is known to respond well to severe pruning, be brave and cut it down almost to ground level – within 30–60cm (12–24in). This hard pruning should be carried out in the winter. In the spring the plant will produce new shoots. For plants that will not tolerate such drastic action, such as many evergreens, do the job over several years, cutting back only one or two of the oldest stems each time. During this renovation remove any dead wood and tie in young replacement stems.

Dead growth

Always cut out dead, dying, diseased and damaged stems as soon as they are noticed, regardless of time of year. Prune the shoots right back to healthy tissue. If you have the time it is always a good idea to remove dead flowers regularly, as not only does this make the plant look tidier, but also often results in more flowers following in the same season. This is certainly true of many climbing roses, for instance. It also reduces the risk of disease moving in to dead areas. However, some climbers are grown for their fruits or attractive seed heads, including various clematis species, so do not dead-head these.

Standard climbers

Some climbers can be grown as standards in large tubs to make unusual patio features. Standards are like small trees, with a single stem and a head of branches at the top. Climbers that are spur pruned, such as grape vines, *Wisteria*, *Solanum crispum* and *S. jasminoides*, are ideal for training as standards, as are *Lonicera* species (honeysuckles) that do not mind regular pruning.

To create a standard, first pot and stake a single-stemmed young plant, then cut back the stem by about one-third. Lateral or side shoots are allowed to grow on this to encourage it to thicken, and are removed gradually over three years, those remaining being shortened by two-thirds in the summer. In the first winter remove the lower third of laterals, in the second winter the middle third and in the third winter the top laterals. Lightly cut back the leading shoot each year, again to help strengthen and thicken the stem. When the desired height is reached, normally about 1.5m (5ft), allow laterals to develop at the top of the stem to form a head of branches.

A WONDERFUL MIXTURE of colours brings life to this classic garden scene. Note how the blooms of the climbing rose combine well with the bed in the foreground and the light brown stone of the house wall. Such roses can be dead-headed through the flowering season to prolong the display.

GLORIOUS YELLOW Clematis tangutica *flowers and frothy foliage merge with flowering plants in a decorative border.*

A LUSH CORNER, brimming with foliage and flowers. The climbing rose and Vitis *vine sweep in from above and complete the picture.*

The procedure for pruning the head of established standards is the same as for climbing plants, and a permanent wooden stake will be needed for support.

PROPAGATION

Propagating your own climbers is an economical way of obtaining new plants. Rooting cuttings is a widely used method, especially where many new plants are required. The same is true of raising plants from seeds, but this method is suitable only for species, not cultivars and hybrids that do not come true to type. Many climbers can be propagated by layering, which involves rooting a stem while it is still attached to the parent plant. This technique is ideal where only a few new plants are needed.

Taking cuttings
Stem cuttings are the most widely used, consisting of a portion of stem in various degrees of ripeness or maturity: one can take softwood, semi-ripe and hardwood cuttings. You need to choose the best type of cutting for the particular plant being propagated.

Softwood cuttings taken in spring and early summer are the most challenging to root because very soft shoots are used, which wilt all too easily. They are suitable for many deciduous climbers. Select new soft shoots 4–5cm (1½–2in) long and cut just below a node or leaf joint at the base. Remove the lower leaves (leave two or three pairs of leaves at the top) and the soft tip, and dip the base of the cutting in hormone rooting powder. Insert in pots of cuttings compost (equal parts peat and coarse sand), water in and place in a heated, humid propagating case with a temperature of 15°C (59°F). The cuttings should develop roots in a few weeks.

Semi-ripe cuttings, taken in mid- to late summer, are also prepared from current season's shoots, but are soft at the tip and hard or ripening at the base. They are suitable for a very wide range of deciduous and evergreen climbers. Cuttings vary in length from 6–10cm (2½–4in) depending on growth. Cut the shoot immediately below a node or leaf joint at the base, remove the lower third of

CLIMBERS FOR TRAINING AS STANDARDS

- *Actinidia kolomikta*
- *Campsis radicans* (Common trumpet creeper)
- X *Fatshedera lizei* (Tree ivy)
- *Hedera helix* (Common or English ivy)
- *Hydrangea anomala* subsp. *petiolaris* (Climbing hydrangea)
- *Lonicera japonica* (Japanese honeysuckle)
- *Lonicera periclymenum* (Common honeysuckle)
- *Schizophragma hydrangeoides*
- *Solanum crispum* (Chilean potato tree)
- *Solanum jasminoides* (Potato vine)
- *Vitis vinifera* (Grape vine)
- *Wisteria floribunda* (Japanese wisteria)
- *Wisteria sinensis* (Chinese wisteria)

leaves and then dip the base of the cutting in hormone rooting powder. Insert the cuttings in pots of cuttings compost, water in and place in a cold frame to root, or in a propagating case if the subject needs heat to root. A humid atmosphere is required for rooting. Cuttings should be rooted by the following growing season.

Hardwood cuttings are prepared from late autumn to mid-winter from current-season's shoots that are fully ripe or hard. They are suitable for various deciduous climbers such as *Vitis* (Grape vines) and *Fallopia baldschuanica*. Select leafless stems and cut them into lengths of 20cm (8in) with secateurs, below a bud at the base and above a bud at the top. Dip in hormone rooting powder, insert in deep pots of cuttings compost and place in a cold frame. Hardwood cuttings are slow rooting, often producing leaves in spring before they have rooted. Allow a year before lifting and planting out. Rooting can be speeded up by placing cuttings in a heated propagating case, as is usually practised with vines.

Leaf-bud cuttings are modified versions of stem cuttings and are useful for several deciduous and evergreen climbers. They can be softwood or semi-ripe. Climbers commonly propagated from leaf-bud cuttings include clematis (softwood or semi-ripe) and ivies (semi-ripe). You get more cuttings from a length stem than with conventional stem cuttings. Each cutting consists of a 2.5cm (1in) length of stem, cut between nodes at the base but just above a node at the top, with a leaf or pair of leaves at the top containing a growth bud in the leaf axil. Otherwise treat leaf-bud cuttings as for softwood or semi-ripe stem cuttings.

Layering

Layering involves encouraging a stem to root while still attached to the plant. It is a suitable and easy method of propagating many deciduous and evergreen climbers such as clematis, wisterias and akebias. Some climbers may self-layer if the stem comes into contact with the soil, such as ivies used as ground cover. Layering is carried out in the spring and stems can take up to a year to root.

Serpentine layering is used for climbers, rooting the stem in a number of places along its length. Use one of the previous year's stems. You need to wound the underside of the stem where you want it to root, by making a slanting cut about 2.5cm (1in) long between nodes to form a tongue. Keep this cut open with a matchstick and dust it with hormone rooting powder. Using a V-shaped wire pin, peg down the stem where wounded into an 8cm (3in) deep depression in the ground and cover with soil. The stem is 'snaked' in and out of the soil, ensuring that at least one bud stays above soil between the wounded areas. An alternative technique is to

BOSTON IVY is being trained against this brick wall, which it will eventually cover. In the meantime it still looks decorative.

A HEAVY SWATHE of star jasmine hangs across the top of this gate and down beside the steps. In full bloom the perfume is all-pervading.

A TRADITIONAL 'English garden' combination of roses, delphiniums and wisteria creates a delightful effect in early summer. Wisteria, a twining climber, is easily trained to any shape desired, on both high and low supports.

wound through nodes or leaf joints, or just behind them, and pin the stem where wounded to the soil surface. Keep layers moist at all times. Lift the new plant when it has rooted and sever from parent plant.

Growing from seeds

Seeds of some climbers need a cold period in winter before they will germinate in the spring, examples being members of the rose family such as climbing roses and cotoneaster. Fleshy fruits and berries of other climbers generally need the same treatment. Sow these as soon as collected in late summer or autumn and stand the pots in a cold place to alternately freeze and thaw throughout winter, a technique known as stratification.

Seeds of other climbers can be sown in spring. Seeds with very hard coats, such as those of the pea family, need to have their coats scarified to allow moisture to penetrate before they will germinate. Rub the seeds between two sheets of sandpaper to scratch the surface, or pour boiling water over them and let them soak for 24 hours.

Sow seeds in pots of soil-based seed compost and for spring sowings cover very lightly with compost, followed by a 12mm ($\frac{1}{2}$in) layer of fine-grade vermiculite (a natural mineral). Seeds to be stratified over winter are also lightly covered with compost followed by a 5mm ($\frac{1}{4}$in) layer of grit. Spring sowings are best germinated in a heated propagating case, a temperature of 15–20°C (59–68°F) being suitable for most subjects.

CONTRASTING COLOURS are used here to great effect. Using Clematis *species and a cultivar with different foliage textures and flower colours makes a lively display – rather like a vertical border.*

ABUTILON MEGAPOTAMICUM
Flowering maple

IN THE RIGHT PLACE this graceful evergreen wall shrub is a fast grower, but it needs a good soil and plenty of sunshine and shelter.

A CONTINUOUS SUPPLY of red and yellow bell-like flowers is produced by this exotic climber throughout summer and into autumn.

FEATURES

Wall shrub

A native of Brazil, this thin-stemmed evergreen or semi-evergreen shrub is fairly hardy. However, it prefers to be grown and trained against a warm sheltered wall or fence for protection from severe weather. The bright green leaves are oval or spear-shaped but the plant is grown primarily for its exotic-looking, symmetrical red and yellow bell-shaped flowers, which are produced continuously throughout summer and into autumn on arching shoots. Height and spread 2m (6ft). This is an ideal plant for a sheltered courtyard garden or other enclosed area. The stems are trained out evenly on the support to form a permanent woody framework.

ABUTILON AT A GLANCE

This wall shrub creates an exotic effect with its masses of colourful bell-shaped flowers. Hardy to –5°C (23°F).

JAN	/	RECOMMENDED VARIETIES
FEB	/	*Abutilon megapotamicum*
MAR	planting	'Variegatum' has yellow and
APR	planting	green variegated foliage.
MAY	/	
JUN	flowering ❀	
JULY	flowering ❀	
AUG	flowering ❀	
SEP	flowering ❀	
OCT	flowering ❀	
NOV	/	
DEC	/	

CONDITIONS

Aspect It should be grown in full sun against a warm sheltered wall or fence.

Site This shrub grows best in reasonably fertile, well-drained soil.

GROWING METHOD

Propagation Sow seeds in the spring and germinate at 15–18°C (59–64°F). Take softwood cuttings in the spring.

Watering Apply water only if the soil starts to dry out in summer.

Feeding Feed annually in the spring with a slow-release fertiliser such as the organic blood, fish and bone.

Problems Generally trouble free out of doors.

FLOWERING/FOLIAGE

Flowers The flowers are produced continuously in summer and autumn.

Foliage This species is evergreen or semi-evergreen but the leaves are not particularly attractive, except in the cultivar 'Variegatum', which has variegated foliage.

PRUNING

Requirements This shrub needs annual pruning to encourage flowering and to prevent congested growth. Cut back old flowered shoots to within two or three buds of the main stems in early spring.

ACTINIDIA KOLOMIKTA

Actinidia

UNUSUAL PINK and white markings on its leaves are what gives this climber charm, but they appear only if it is grown in plenty of sun.

A STUNNING PLANT for covering walls and pergolas, this deciduous twiner will need training in the early stages of growth.

FEATURES

Twiner

This strong-growing deciduous climber from eastern Asia has large oval leaves, the lower half deep green and the upper half boldly marked with pink and white. When in full leaf in the spring and summer it creates a distinctly exotic effect. The colours do not form on young plants or old plants kept in shade. It grows to at least 5m (15ft) in height with a spread of about half this. Actinidia is suitable for growing on a large wall or up a large mature tree. It will also work well with a large pergola. If not given sufficient space it will need trimming to keep it within bounds.

ACTINIDIA AT A GLANCE

One of the finest foliage climbers with large, multi-coloured leaves. Hardy to –15°C (5°F).

JAN	/
FEB	planting
MAR	planting
APR	planting
MAY	foliage
JUN	foliage
JULY	foliage
AUG	foliage
SEP	foliage
OCT	/
NOV	/
DEC	/

COMPANION PLANTS

Grow with other exotic-looking climbers such as *Abutilon megapotamicum*

CONDITIONS

Aspect This climber grows best in a sunny position that is well sheltered from strong winds.

Site The soil should be well-drained and rich.

GROWING METHOD

Propagation Sow seeds in autumn and stratify over winter. Take semi-ripe cuttings in summer. Layer stems in the spring.

Watering Apply water only when the soil starts to dry out in the summer.

Feeding Apply slow-release fertilizer once a year in the spring, such as blood, fish and bone mixture.

Problems Not usually troubled by pests or diseases.

FLOWERING/FOLIAGE

Flowers Clusters of white, scented flowers in early summer are followed by yellowish oval fruits on female plant (plants of both sexes are needed for fruit production).

Foliage This climber is grown primarily for its attractive variegated foliage.

PRUNING

Requirements Trim in late winter or early spring if necessary to keep the plant within its allotted space. The plant may eventually need some of the oldest stems thinning out, or renovation pruning.

AKEBIA QUINATA
Chocolate vine

THE CHOCOLATE VINE is not over-vigorous but this particular vine is producing a great show of flowers. It is hard to describe their colour but it is a dark pinkish or purplish brown, and they have an unusual chocolate smell. Leaves consist of five deep green leaflets.

FEATURES

Twiner

The fascinating and unusual purple-brown flowers of the Chocolate vine, a native of China, Japan and Korea, have a light but distinctive smell of chocolate. The foliage is also decorative, and therefore this climber looks good even when not in flower. It is a long-lived twining semi-evergreen climber capable of growing up to 10m (30ft), although it may be less in some gardens. Growth is fairly vigorous once the plant is established but it is rather open in habit and never ends up looking heavy. This climber is seen to best advantage when grown over a trellis screen, pergola or arch, and is also a suitable subject for growing into a large tree.

AKEBIA QUINATA AT A GLANCE

One of the earliest climbers to flower, with unusual chocolate-scented blooms. Hardy to −15°C (5°F).

JAN	/	COMPANION PLANTS
FEB	planting 🖐	Strong-growing summer-flowering clematis or climbing roses will take over from the spring display.
MAR	flowering ❀	
APR	flowering ❀	
MAY	flowering ❀	
JUN	/	
JULY	/	
AUG	/	
SEP	/	
OCT	/	
NOV	/	
DEC	/	

CONDITIONS

Aspect Akebia will grow equally well in full sun or partial shade.

Site The soil must be well-drained, moisture-retentive and reasonably fertile.

GROWING METHOD

Propagation Sow seeds in autumn and place in a cold frame. Take semi-ripe cuttings in summer. Carry out serpentine layering in the spring.

Watering Make sure the soil does not dry in the summer.

Feeding This is necessary only once a year in spring. Apply a slow-release organic fertilizer such as blood, fish and bone.

Problems Not troubled by pests or diseases.

FLOWERING/FOLIAGE

Flowers The scented flowers are produced throughout spring and followed by long fleshy fruits. Warm conditions throughout spring and summer are necessary for fruit to be produced.

Foliage The foliage consists of five deep green leaflets. Leaves may become flushed with an attractive purple colour in the winter.

PRUNING

Requirements If necessary trim the plant after flowering to keep it within bounds. It may eventually need some of the oldest stems thinned out, or renovation pruning.

AMPELOPSIS GLANDULOSA
Ampelopsis

THE VARIEGATED leaves of this Ampelopsis glandulosa *var.* brevipedunculata *'Elegans' create a fascinating texture.*

THE DAPPLED FOLIAGE of A. g. var. b. 'Elegans', makes it a highly effective and decorative wall-covering climber.

FEATURES

Tendril climber

This species is a vigorous deciduous climber from north-east Asia with three-lobed deep green leaves colouring well in autumn. The cultivar *A. glandulosa* var. *brevipedunculata* 'Elegans' is even more attractive as its foliage is variegated pink and white. This cultivar is less vigorous than the species, growing to a height of about 3m (10ft). Ampelopsis support themselves with tendrils and are good climbers for walls and fences, substantial pergolas, or for growing up into large mature trees. Due to its more restrained habit, 'Elegans' is particularly recommended for growing on a pergola over a patio and it could even be tried in a tub.

AMPELOPSIS AT A GLANCE

Tendril climber grown for its pleasant variegated foliage. Hardy to temperatures of −15°C (5°F)

JAN	/	RECOMMENDED VARIETIES
FEB	planting	*A. glandulosa* var.
MAR	planting	*maximowiczii* has variable
APR	planting	foliage, often deeply lobed.
MAY	foliage	
JUN	foliage	
JULY	foliage	
AUG	foliage	
SEP	foliage	
OCT	foliage	
NOV	/	
DEC	/	

CONDITIONS

Aspect   Partial shade is best for 'Elegans' but the species will take sun. Shelter from cold winds.
Site   For best growth provide well-drained yet moisture-retentive and reasonably rich soil.

GROWING METHOD

Propagation Sow seeds in autumn and stratify over winter. Take cuttings in spring or early summer.
Watering   Only needs to be watered if the soil starts to dry out in the summer.
Feeding   As it likes reasonably fertile conditions, feed with a slow-release fertilizer in the spring.
Problems   There are no problems from pests or diseases.

FLOWERING/FOLIAGE

Flowers   The tiny green flowers in summer are not particularly showy but may be followed, after a long hot summer, by attractive blue berries, provided the plant is growing in full sun.
Foliage   Ampelopsis is essentially a foliage climber and the cultivar 'Elegans' is particularly attractive.

PRUNING

Requirements Trim in spring if necessary to keep it within bounds. This climber can also be spur pruned in late winter. Thinning or renovation pruning may eventually be needed.

ARISTOLOCHIA
Dutchman's pipe

THE VIGOROUS Aristolochia littoralis *swathes itself effectively from the roof support of a conservatory, creating an exotic scene.*

ARISTOLOCHIA FLOWERS are strangely beautiful and intriguing objects. They might need to be encouraged from under the dense foliage.*

FEATURES

Twiner

Aristolochia macrophylla is a deciduous climber from the south-east USA. It has very unusual pipe- or siphon-shaped flowers in summer. These are green, strikingly marked with brown, purple and yellow. The foliage is also very attractive so the plant looks good all through spring and summer. It is a strong grower and in good conditions can reach a height of 10m (30ft), but in some gardens it may be considerably less. Another aristolochia is *A. littoralis*, which can only be grown in a warm greenhouse or conservatory. You will need plenty of space to grow Dutchman's pipe, such as a high wall or fence.

ARISTOLOCHIA AT A GLANCE

An exotic-looking climber with bizarre flowers and attractive heart-shaped leaves. Hardy to −5°C (23°F).

JAN	/	COMPANION PLANTS
FEB	/	It needs an equally vigorous
MAR	/	companion. For a long
APR	planting 🌱	period of interest, try it with
MAY	planting 🌱	wisteria, which flowers
JUN	flowering ✽	before aristolochia, in spring.
JULY	flowering ✽	
AUG	flowering ✽	
SEP	/	
OCT	/	
NOV	/	
DEC	/	

CONDITIONS

Aspect   This climber will grow well in full sun or partial shade.

Site   The soil should be well-drained and reasonably rich. Even a dryish soil is suitable.

GROWING METHOD

Propagation   Sow seeds in spring and germinate at 16°C (61°F). Take softwood cuttings in summer.

Watering   Only apply water if the soil is drying out in the summer. It likes to be on the dry side throughout the winter.

Feeding   Do not over-feed, as this is a naturally vigorous climber. A slow-release organic fertilizer applied each spring will be sufficient.

Problems   Not usually troubled by pests or diseases.

FLOWERING/FOLIAGE

Flowers   Grown mainly for its flowers but unfortunately they are inclined to be obscured from view by the plant's lush foliage.

Foliage   The large, heart shaped, deep green leaves are very attractive.

PRUNING

Requirements   This climber can either be spur pruned in early spring, or simply trimmed in spring to keep it within bounds, but eventually it will need thinning or renovation pruning.

BERBERIDOPSIS CORALLINA

Coral vine

THE INTENSE SCARLET of these Berberidopsis corallina *flowers makes up for their small size, and they blaze amid the rich foliage.*

THE DEEP GREEN foliage of B. corallina *makes a marvellous background for the vibrant flowers.*

FEATURES

Twiner

A spectacular evergreen climber from Chile, valued for its exotic-looking pendulous red flowers, and ideal for a shady wall or fence. It can be especially recommended for a shady courtyard that is well protected from cold winds, but it also looks at home in a woodland garden, with suitable perennials and shrubs, as it grows in woodland in the wild. The Coral vine can also be grown through large shrubs or up mature trees. It can reach a height of up to 5m (15ft). A severe winter may kill back the stems but it may still go on to produce new shoots from the base in the spring.

CONDITIONS

Aspect   The Coral vine needs a position in shade or

BERBERIDOPSIS AT A GLANCE

Pendulous red flowers and deep green spiny foliage. Hardy to temperatures of −5°C (23°F).

JAN	/	
FEB	/	
MAR	/	
APR	planting	
MAY	planting	
JUN	flowering	
JULY	flowering	
AUG	flowering	
SEP	flowering	
OCT	/	
NOV	/	
DEC	/	

COMPANION PLANTS
Looks good with x *Fatshedera lizei*, which will also take shade. Also woodland-garden shrubs and perennials, including ferns.

Site   partial shade, with shelter from cold winds. The soil must be acid or neutral, contain plenty of humus, and be able to retain moisture yet well drained. A deep organic mulch applied in autumn will protect the roots from severe frosts. Coral vine grows best on wire or trellis but will also scramble over fences, tree stumps and other objects.

GROWING METHOD

Propagation   Sow seeds in spring and germinate in a cold frame. Carry out serpentine layering in spring. Take semi-ripe cuttings towards the end of summer.

Watering   Do not allow the plant to dry out at any time. Keep the soil steadily moist.

Feeding   Once a year in spring, using a slow-release fertilizer, but avoid alkaline types.

Problems   Neither pests nor diseases are a problem.

FLOWERING/FOLIAGE

Flowers   Long-stalked pendulous flowers are carried in rows on the shoots.

Foliage   Elliptical deep green leaves have spiny edges and grey-green undersides.

PRUNING

Requirements   Minimal pruning is needed for this climber. It is best not to prune unless it is considered essential. The Coral vine certainly does not like hard cutting back. Spring is the best time for pruning, removing dead growth and any very weak stems. Eventually, as the plant matures, some judicious thinning may be necessary.

CAMPSIS RADICANS
Trumpet creeper

THE SHEER VIGOUR *of* Campsis radicans *is evident as its abundant growth dominates a sizeable house wall.*

IN CLOSE-UP *the texture-enhancing serrate edges and glossy surfaces of* C. radicans' *leaves are clearly visible.*

FEATURES

Self-clinging climber

The Trumpet creeper is a flamboyant deciduous climber from the south-east USA, bearing rich orange trumpet-shaped flowers in late summer and into autumn and attractive ferny foliage. The stems produce aerial roots so when this climber is well established it is self-supporting. But bear in mind that it is very vigorous, growing to at least 10m (30ft) tall. Grow it on a high wall (it is a good subject for a sheltered courtyard garden), over a large outbuilding or up a mature tree. Campsis can also be grown in a tub and trained as a standard to make an unusual feature on a warm sunny patio.

CAMPSIS RADICANS AT A GLANCE

An exotic-looking climber with orange trumpet-shaped flowers and attractive ferny foliage. Hardy to –5°C (23°F).

JAN	/	RECOMMENDED VARIETIES
FEB	/	*C. radicans* f. *flava* has
MAR	planting ✤	pleasant yellow flowers.
APR	planting ✤	
MAY	/	
JUN	/	
JULY	/	
AUG	flowering ✿	
SEP	flowering ✿	
OCT	flowering ✿	
NOV	/	
DEC	/	

CONDITIONS

Aspect   This climber needs to be protected from cold winds. Placing it in full sun will ensure optimum flowering.

Site   Grow it in reasonably rich, well-drained, yet moisture-retentive soil.

GROWING METHOD

Propagation   Sow seeds in spring and germinate at 16°C (61°F). Take semi-ripe cuttings in summer or hardwood cuttings in late autumn or winter. Carry out serpentine layering in spring.

Watering   Water in summer if the soil is drying out.

Feeding   Once a year, in spring, apply a slow-release organic fertilizer such as blood, fish and bone.

Problems   Campsis can suffer from scale insects and powdery mildew.

FLOWERING/FOLIAGE

Flowers   Clusters of exotic trumpet-shaped flowers.

Foliage   It produces attractive pinnate or ferny looking deep green leaves.

PRUNING

Requirements   Annual spur pruning in late winter or early spring, cutting back side shoots to two or three buds. If renovation pruning is needed the entire plant can be cut back hard – to within 30–45cm (12–18in) of the ground.

CELASTRUS ORBICULATUS
Oriental bittersweet

A VIGOROUS AND TOLERANT climber, Celastrus orbiculatus has been used here to great effect as a lush covering for a high wall.

THESE MELLOW AUTUMN FRUITS are starting to swell, and will soon burst open to display the vivid scarlet or pink seeds inside.

FEATURES

I winer

Also known as the Staff vine, this is a deciduous climber from eastern Asia, grown primarily for its spectacular fruits that are produced in autumn. These are yellow, but eventually open up to reveal striking red or pink seeds. You either need to plant both sexes together or grow an hermaphrodite form for fruit production. This celastrus is very vigorous, growing to a height of 14m (45ft) and it needs plenty of room to grow. It can be recommended for growing on a high wall (be wary about training it on the house walls), over a large outbuilding or up a mature tree.

CELASTRUS AT A GLANCE

Valued for its display of autumnal fruits and leaf tints. Hardy to temperatures of −15°C (5°F).

JAN	/	RECOMMENDED VARIETIES
FEB	planting 🌿	'Diana' (female)
MAR	planting 🌿	'Hercules' (male)
APR	planting 🌿	Hermaphrodite Group
MAY	/	
JUN	/	
JULY	/	
AUG	/	
SEP	fruits 🍂	
OCT	fruits 🍂	
NOV	/	
DEC	/	

CONDITIONS

Aspect	The Oriental bittersweet is best in full sun but it will thrive in a position with partial shade.
Site	It needs a well-drained soil.

GROWING METHOD

Propagation	Sow seeds in autumn and stratify over winter. Take softwood cuttings in spring or early summer, or semi-ripe cuttings in late summer. Serpentine layering in spring.
Watering	Only needs to be watered if the soil starts to become very dry in summer.
Feeding	An annual spring application of slow-release organic fertilizer is all that's needed.
Problems	There are no problems from pests or diseases.

FLOWERING/FOLIAGE

Flowers	Tiny green flowers are produced in summer, followed by a spectacular display of fruits.
Foliage	The elliptic to rounded leaves turn yellow in autumn before they fall.

PRUNING

Requirements	Prune in late winter or early spring, but it does not need regular pruning. Cut back extra-vigorous shoots if necessary. The plant may eventually need thinning out, removing some of the oldest stems by cutting them back to within 45cm (18in) of the ground.

CHAENOMELES SPECIOSA
Flowering quince

THERE IS A DEEP GLOSSY SHEEN to the oval leaves, which usually emerge after the flowers have bloomed on the bare branches.

THIS ADAPTABLE PLANT makes a good hedge, does well in a flower border and can be trained to grow up a sunny wall.

FEATURES

Wall shrub

This deciduous spiny shrub, a native of China, is very amenable to training flat against a wall or fence. The spines and thick growth of this plant make it a practical barrier shrub – and it can also be trained as a hedge. It flowers only from young shoots, so build up a system of permanent stems, tying them in to their support, and the flowers will be produced on the previous year's side shoots. The rich red blooms appear in spring, often very early in the season. Although of vigorous habit, growing up to 2.5m (8ft) high with a spread of 5m (15ft), it is ideally suited to growing on a wall of the house, or on a fence of normal height, as it can be kept smaller if desired by pruning.

CHAENOMELES AT A GLANCE

A spiny shrub with cup-shaped flowers, often on bare stems, in the spring. Hardy to −15°C (5°F).

		RECOMMENDED VARIETIES
JAN	/	'Geisha Girl', double, deep apricot
FEB	planting 🖐	
MAR	planting 🖐	'Moerloosei', white and pink
APR	flowering ❋	'Nivalis', white
MAY	flowering ❋	'Simonii', double, deep red
JUN	/	
JULY	/	
AUG	/	
SEP	/	
OCT	/	
NOV	/	
DEC	/	

CONDITIONS

Aspect The Flowering quince should be grown in full sun or partial shade. However, flowering is most prolific in sun.

Site This shrub will thrive in any well-drained soil that is reasonably fertile.

GROWING METHOD

Propagation Sow seeds in autumn and stratify them over winter. Take semi-ripe cuttings in summer.

Watering Watering is only needed if the soil starts to dry out excessively in the summer.

Feeding In the spring apply a slow-release organic fertilizer such as blood, fish and bone.

Problems The plant may be attacked by pests including aphids and scale insects.

FLOWERING/FOLIAGE

Flowers Bowl-shaped flowers, which are usually red with yellow anthers, are produced in the spring. They are followed by fragrant, apple-shaped, greenish yellow edible fruits, which can be used to make jelly.

Foliage The oval leaves are shiny and deep green.

PRUNING

Requirements Build up a permanent framework of stems and then spur prune annually after flowering – cut back the old flowered shoots to within two to four buds of the framework.

CLEMATIS
Clematis species and cultivars

THE FIRST FLOWER of this C. montana *cultivar is fully open and the plump buds promise more in the near future.*

C. armandii *'Apple Blossom' is a vigorous spring-flowering evergreen that needs to be grown in a warm, sheltered position.*

FLOWERS of the Jackmanii hybrids are by far the largest of all cultivated clematis. These large lavender-blue ones are quite lovely.

FEATURES

Twiner

There are at least 200 species, deciduous and evergreen, and countless cultivars and hybrids of clematis, the most popular of all climbers. They are native mostly to the northern hemisphere, and the British native is *Clematis vitalba* (Traveller's joy, Old man's beard), which sprawls over hedgerows and produces greeny white flowers in summer followed by silky seed heads. This is not generally grown in gardens as it is not sufficiently decorative. The many other species, cultivars and hybrids are more preferable.

The deciduous spring-flowering *C. montana* and its cultivars are especially popular, with flowers in white or in shades of pink. *C. armandii* and its cultivar 'Apple Blossom' are vigorous spring-flowering evergreens, with white and pink-tinged flowers respectively.

The large-flowered hybrids are the most popular of all, flowering in the summer. They have some of the most spectacular flowers imaginable. All are deciduous and of modest growth. They come in a range of colours, including white, blue, purple, mauve and red shades, and some are bicoloured. Perhaps the best known is 'Jackmanii' with deep purple flowers.

Tall clematis such as *C. montana* are often allowed to climb into mature trees where their flowers tumble out over the canopy. Less-vigorous clematis, such as the large-flowered hybrids, are excellent for walls, fences, pergolas, arches, arbours, obelisks and tubs. Thin stemmed, light and airy clematis, such as the Viticella Group, are ideal for growing over large shrubs or for use as ground cover. They are also good for containers.

CONDITIONS

Aspect   Clematis like to have their top growth in full sun but their roots in the shade. Roots can be shaded with plantings of ground-cover plants or with other low-growing subjects, with paving slabs or with even a deep mulch of organic matter.

Site   Clematis grow well in any well-drained, reasonably rich soil containing plenty of humus. They are particularly suitable for chalky soils. Keep the plants permanently mulched with organic matter.

GROWING METHOD

Propagation   Sow seeds as soon as collected in the autumn and stratify them over winter. They should then go on to germinate in the spring. Take softwood or semi-ripe leaf-bud cuttings in spring or summer. Carry out serpentine layering in the spring.

THIS TRANQUIL RURAL VIEW is beautifully framed by a fence covered with a rambling Clematis montana. *The delicate tracery of the stems and the scattering of white flowers would be just as attractive in a city garden.*

Watering Clematis should not be allowed to suffer from lack of moisture, so water plants well during rainless periods if the soil starts to dry out.

Feeding An annual application of slow-release organic fertilizer, such as blood, fish and bone, should be applied in the spring.

Problems Clematis wilt is the biggest problem. To help overcome this disease, plant clematis deeply, covering the top of the rootball with 8cm (3in) of soil. This also ensures that new stems grow from below ground. Aphids may infest plants in the summer.

FLOWERING/FOLIAGE

Flowers Clematis flower mainly in the spring, summer and autumn, according to type. A few species bloom in the winter. Flowers come in all colours and they may be flat, bell-shaped or cup-shaped.

Foliage This may be deciduous or evergreen, according to the individual species. Generally the leaves have twining stalks.

PRUNING

Requirements Pruning varies according to the group that clematis are in. Group 1 contains clematis that flower early in the year on previous year's shoots, including *C. montana* and cultivars, *C. alpina*, *C. cirrhosa* var. *balearica*, *C. macropetala*, and *C. armandii*. The only pruning these plants need is thinning when they become congested. This is done after flowering. If renovation pruning is needed, cut down the complete plant to within 30cm (12in) of the ground after flowering.

Group 2 contains large-flowered hybrids that produce a flush of flowers in early summer on last-year's shoots, and then another flush of blooms in late summer and autumn on current year's shoots. These are pruned in late winter or early spring. Established plants can get by with very little pruning. The simplest technique is to cut them to within about 30cm (12in) of the ground, every three to four years. After pruning you will lose the early summer flowers but they will bloom in late summer.

Group 3 contains clematis that flower in late summer and early autumn on current season's shoots. This growth comes from the base of the plant. Included in this group are *C. viticella* and its cultivars and hybrids, *C. orientalis*, and 'Jackmanii'. Plants are pruned annually in late winter or early spring down to within 30cm (12in) of the ground.

CLEMATIS AT A GLANCE

Very variable climbers, suitable for many situations. Flat, bell-shaped or cup-shaped flowers. Most are hardy to −15°C (5°F).

JAN	/	RECOMMENDED VARIETIES
FEB	planting ✍	Other clematis worth
MAR	planting ✍	growing:
APR	flowering ✽	*C. alpina*, blue flowers,
MAY	flowering ✽	spring
JUN	flowering ✽	*C. cirrhosa* var. *balearica*,
JULY	flowering ✽	cream, winter/spring
AUG	flowering ✽	*C. macropetala*, blue, spring
SEP	flowering ✽	*C. orientalis*, yellow, summer
OCT	flowering ✽	*C. tangutica*, yellow,
NOV	/	summer/autumn
DEC	/	

CLIANTHUS PUNICEUS
Glory pea

IN AREAS SUBJECT to hard frosts in winter, grow Clianthus puniceus *in a cool conservatory or greenhouse.*

AS WELL AS its eyecatching red blooms in spring, C. puniceus *is grown for the all-year interest of its attractive pinnate leaves.*

FEATURES

Scrambler

This flamboyant semi-evergreen or evergreen climber will provide a touch of the southern hemisphere, as it is a native of the north island of New Zealand. Flowering in spring and early summer, it produces clusters of unusual, scarlet, claw-like flowers, another of its popular names being Lobster claw. These flowers are the plant's principal attraction. It will grow up to 4m (12ft) tall and needs to be grown against a warm sheltered wall. When grown unsupported it tends to spread horizontally. The Glory pea is an ideal subject for a small courtyard or other enclosed area. In parts of the country that are subject to hard frosts, it would be better to grow this climber in a frost-free conservatory or glasshouse.

CLIANTHUS AT A GLANCE

Scarlet claw-like flowers and handsome pinnate foliage. Hardy to temperatures of –5°C (23°F).

JAN	/	RECOMMENDED VARIETIES
FEB	/	'Albus', white flowers
MAR	/	'Roseus', deep rose-pink
APR	planting 🖐	flowers
MAY	flowering ❀	
JUN	flowering ❀	
JULY	/	
AUG	/	
SEP	/	
OCT	/	
NOV	/	
DEC	/	

CONDITIONS

Aspect   It must have a position in full sun and be well sheltered from cold winds.

Site   The soil should be very well drained. This climber will thrive in quite poor soils. A deep permanent mulch of organic matter is recommended to protect roots from frost.

GROWING METHOD

Propagation   Take softwood or semi-ripe cuttings in spring or summer. Sow seeds in spring, first soaking them in water or abrading them (see pages 62–63). Germinate at 18°C (64°F).

Watering   Fairly drought tolerant but apply water if the soil dries out excessively in the summer.

Feeding   Give an annual spring application of a general purpose slow-release organic fertilizer, such as blood, fish and bone.

Problems   There are no problems from pests or diseases.

FLOWERING/FOLIAGE

Flowers   Valued for its early, exotic-looking flowers.

Foliage   The shiny pinnate leaves are attractive.

PRUNING

Requirements   Very little needed. This climber will not survive severe pruning. Cut out any weak or dead shoots as necessary. Stems may be killed back by hard frosts, but the plant may produce new shoots from the base in spring. Cut back dead growth to live tissue.

COTONEASTER
Fishbone cotoneaster

COTONEASTERS ARE *positively weighed down by a mass of scarlet berries in the autumn. This species is* C. horizontalis.

PINK AND WHITE FLOWERS *stud the stiff branches of this* Cotoneaster horizontalis. *It requires very little care.*

FEATURES

Wall Shrub

Cotoneaster horizontalis is a deciduous shrub native to western China. It is not actually a true climber but it can be trained flat against a wall. The branches resemble fishbones in formation, hence the common name. This shrub is grown primarily for its masses of red berries in the autumn that last well into winter, provided birds leave them alone. Autumnal leaf tints considerably enhance the display of berries. It can be trained to a height of at least 1.5m (5ft) with a similar spread, and is a good plant for a house wall or a fence. The Fishbone cotoneaster also makes an excellent ground-cover plant.

COTONEASTER AT A GLANCE

Deciduous shrub with a fishbone arrangement of branches. Heavy crop of red berries in autumn. Hardy to −15°C (5°F).

JAN	/	COMPANION PLANTS
FEB	planting 🌱	Looks especially good
MAR	planting 🌱	growing with ivies (hederas)
APR	planting 🌱	or *Jasminum nudiflorum*
MAY	flowering ❀	(Winter jasmine). If used as
JUN	flowering ❀	ground cover, try combining
JULY	/	it with prostrate junipers
AUG	/	(*Juniperus* species)
SEP	fruits 🍂	
OCT	fruits 🍂	
NOV	fruits 🍂	
DEC	fruits 🍂	

CONDITIONS

Aspect Provide a position in full sun for best flowering and fruiting.

Site Grows in any well-drained, reasonably rich soil. Tolerates dry conditions.

GROWING METHOD

Propagation Sow seeds in autumn and stratify over winter. Take semi-ripe cuttings in summer.

Watering You only need apply water if the soil starts to dry out excessively in the summer.

Feeding Apply a slow-release organic fertilizer, such as blood, fish and bone, in the spring each year.

Problems This shrub can become infested with aphids and scale insects.

FLOWERING/FOLIAGE

Flowers Produces an abundant mass of small white flowers in late spring.

Foliage Small, rounded, deep green shiny leaves which turn red in autumn before they fall.

PRUNING

Requirements This plant does not need regular pruning. However, it can be trimmed back in late winter or early spring to keep it within its allotted space. Spread out and tie in the stems as necessary. They can be trained perfectly flat against the wall or fence.

DECUMARIA BARBARA
Decumaria

APPEARING IN EARLY summer, the delightful puffs of cream-coloured sweetly-scented flowers are the main attraction of Decumaria barbara. *This plants is a sturdy climber and can easily scale and cover large walls and substantial trees.*

FEATURES

Self-clinging climber

This deciduous climber from the south-east USA has stems that produce aerial roots, so eventually it is self-supporting. Decumaria is grown for its flat heads of fragrant, cream flowers that are produced in early summer. Attaining a height of 10m (30ft), it is ideal for growing up a tall mature tree or high wall. Be wary about growing this climber on a house wall, as it will be impossible to remove it for house maintenance without damaging the stems. There is also the risk of damaging the wall itself. This plant makes good and unusual groundcover in a woodland garden or shrub border. It will also enjoy the partial or dappled shade of these situations.

DECUMARIA AT A GLANCE

A self-clinging climber with flat heads of cream flowers and handsome glossy foliage. Hardy to −5°C (23°F).

JAN	/	COMPANION PLANTS
FEB	/	Looks good with climbing
MAR	planting ✤	roses, which should flower at
APR	planting ✤	the same time.
MAY	/	
JUN	flowering ❀	
JULY	/	
AUG	/	
SEP	/	
OCT	/	
NOV	/	
DEC	/	

CONDITIONS

Aspect Grows well in full sun or partial shade. Provide shelter from cold drying winds as this climber is not fully hardy and may therefore be damaged in an exposed situation.

Site Any well-drained fertile soil will be suitable for this climber.

GROWING METHOD

Propagation Take semi-ripe cuttings in late summer. When grown as ground cover it will self-layer, so simply remove rooted portions of stem, complete with buds or young shoots, if new plants are required.

Watering If the soil starts to dry out in summer water the plant well. It dislikes drying out.

Feeding An annual spring application of slow-release fertilizer, such as the organic blood, fish and bone, will be sufficient.

Problems Not troubled by pests or diseases.

FLOWERING/FOLIAGE

Flowers The cream flowers, which are produced in early summer, smell of honey.

Foliage The large deep green leaves are attractive and make a good background for the flowers.

PRUNING

Requirements No regular pruning needed. If necessary trim after flowering to keep within allotted space.

EUONYMUS FORTUNEI
Euonymus

MANY CULTIVARS of Euonymus fortunei *have variegated leaves, and here a delicate white edging lightens the dense growth.*

THE LEAVES of this E. f. *'Emerald 'n' Gold' are among the brightest of all the cultivars.*

FEATURES

Scrambler

This is an evergreen shrub that will climb to 5m (15ft) if grown against a wall or fence. It also makes excellent ground cover in a shrub border or on a bank. The species, which is a native of China, is not normally grown, but rather the many cultivars, which may have either plain green or variegated foliage. It is an excellent choice if a moderately vigorous climber is needed for the house walls, and it does not mind being trimmed back to keep it within bounds. *Euonymus fortunei* can also be trained up a mature tree or through a large shrub. The plant does have a crop of pink fruit, but these are rarely produced in northern climates, including Britain.

EUONYMUS AT A GLANCE

Climbing or ground-cover shrub with plain green or variegated evergreen foliage. Hardy to –15°C (5°F).

JAN	foliage 🌱	RECOMMENDED VARIETIES
FEB	planting 🌿	'Coloratus', deep green
MAR	planting 🌿	'Dart's Blanket', deep green
APR	planting 🌿	'Emerald Gaiety', bright
MAY	foliage 🌱	green, white edges
JUN	foliage 🌱	'Emerald 'n' Gold', bright
JULY	foliage 🌱	green and yellow
AUG	foliage 🌱	'Kewensis', deep green
SEP	foliage 🌱	'Silver Queen', white-edged
OCT	foliage 🌱	leaves
NOV	foliage 🌱	'Sunspot', deep green, with
DEC	foliage 🌱	central golden spot

CONDITIONS

Aspect Full sun, especially for the variegated cultivars that then colour up really well. Partial shade also suitable.

Site This euonymus grows in any well-drained soil but is especially good for poor soils.

GROWING METHOD

Propagation Take semi-ripe cuttings in late summer. Ground-cover plants can be layered. They may even self-layer.

Watering This shrub tolerates fairly dry conditions, but it is advisable to water well if the soil starts to dry out excessively in summer.

Feeding Apply a slow-release organic fertilizer, such as blood, fish and bone, in the spring.

Problems Plants may be attacked by scale insects, caterpillars and vine weevil beetles.

FLOWERING/FOLIAGE

Flowers These are insignificant – the plant is grown for its foliage.

Foliage Evergreen oval or elliptic leaves, plain green or variegated according to cultivar.

PRUNING

Requirements Does not need regular pruning. Train in the young stems to cover the support and trim in early spring if necessary to keep the plant within its allotted space.

FALLOPIA BALDSCHUANICA
Russian vine

A WAVE OF the exceptionally vigorous Fallopia baldschuanica, *vibrant with white flowers, overcomes a garden wall and door.*

THE LIVELY TEXTURE of F. baldschuanica *is largely created by its stems of white flowers as they twist to point up toward the sky.*

FEATURES

Twiner

The other popular name for this deciduous climber, Mile-a-minute plant, sums up its habit of growth. It is extremely vigorous, even rampant, and grows up to 12m (40ft) tall. Grow this plant only if you have plenty of room for it to take off, otherwise you will be forever cutting it back to keep it in check. It is best suited to informal or wild gardens where it can be left to 'run free'. Its rampant nature also makes it ideal for filling a space or even hiding an unsightly structure in the garden. The Russian vine is originally a native of eastern Europe and Iran. From late summer and into autumn it is covered in a froth of small white, pink-flushed flowers that hang in decorative swags. It is ideal for quickly covering large outbuildings, or for growing up very high walls or large mature trees.

FALLOPIA AT A GLANCE

One of the fastest-growing climbers available, it has luxuriant leafy growth and a froth of white flowers. Hardy to −15°C (5°F).

JAN	/	
FEB	planting 🌱	
MAR	planting 🌱	
APR	planting 🌱	
MAY	/	
JUN	/	
JULY	/	
AUG	flowering ❁	
SEP	flowering ❁	
OCT	flowering ❁	
NOV	/	
DEC	/	

COMPANION PLANTS
As it is such a large vigorous plant, this climber is best grown alone.

CONDITIONS

Aspect Suitable for full sun or partial shade.
Site Any soil, even poor conditions. However, the soil should be moisture retentive yet well drained.

GROWING METHOD

Propagation Take softwood or semi-ripe cuttings in spring and summer, or hardwood cuttings in late autumn or winter. Hardwood cuttings are easier to root than other types and should be rooted in a frost-free glasshouse.
Watering If the soil starts to dry out excessively in summer, water heavily.
Feeding It does not need much encouragement to grow, but can be given a slow-release organic fertilizer in spring.
Problems Not usually troubled by pests or diseases.

FLOWERING/FOLIAGE

Flowers The plant flowers very freely and looks its best when covered in a froth of white blossom.
Foliage The deep green leaves are heart shaped.

PRUNING

Requirements It can be allowed to grow without pruning as it forms a tangled mass of stems. If you need to restrict growth, prune back stems by one-third, using shears. If the plant needs renovating, cut it down to within 90cm (3ft) of the ground. This will result in vigorous new growth. The time to prune is late winter or early spring.

X FATSHEDERA LIZEI
Tree ivy

THE STUNNING LEAVES of X Fatshedera lizei *are evergreen, and very deply lobed. Being deep green and very shiny they create a luxuriant effect in any garden. The Tree ivy can be grown as a climber, as groundcover, or even as a standard in a tub.*

FEATURES

Scrambler

An evergreen shrub of spreading habit. It is not a true climber but can be trained against a wall, on an obelisk, or as a standard in a tub. The Tree ivy also makes good ground cover. It is a hybrid of *Fatsia* and *Hedera* (ivy) that originated under cultivation, and has the characteristics of both parents. The Tree ivy is valued for its lush foliage that looks good all the year round. Highly adaptable, it is a very good choice for shady town and city gardens, and takes atmospheric pollution in its stride. The plant is of modest stature, growing to a height of 1.2–1.8m (4–6ft), or more when trained to a support.

X FATSHEDERA LIZEI AT A GLANCE

An ivy-like shrub with lustrous dark green foliage. Hardy to –5°C (23°F).

JAN	foliage 🌿	RECOMMENDED VARIETIES
FEB	foliage 🌿	'Annemieke', yellow
MAR	foliage 🌿	variegated leaves
APR	planting 🌱	'Variegata', white-edged
MAY	planting 🌱	leaves
JUN	foliage 🌿	These two are half-hardy and
JULY	foliage 🌿	should be grown in pots
AUG	foliage 🌿	under glass.
SEP	flowering ✿	
OCT	flowering ✿	
NOV	foliage 🌿	
DEC	foliage 🌿	

CONDITIONS

Aspect   Good for partial shade but also grows well in a sunny spot.

Site   Thrives in any soil. The ideal soil is reasonably rich, moisture-retentive yet well-drained.

GROWING METHOD

Propagation   Take semi-ripe leaf-bud cuttings in summer. Stems can also be layered.

Watering   Keep the soil moist in summer during dry spells as the plant dislikes drying out.

Feeding   Give an annual spring application of slow-release organic fertilizer such as blood, fish and bone.

Problems   Generally free from pests and diseases.

FLOWERING/FOLIAGE

Flowers   Heads of tiny green-white flowers are produced in autumn. These are not the most showy of flowers and the plant is grown primarily for its decorative foliage.

Foliage   The evergreen deeply lobed leaves are deep green and shiny, creating a luxuriant effect.

PRUNING

Requirements   Does not need pruning, only the removal or cutting back of any shoots that spoil the overall shape. Pruning should be carried out in late winter or early spring.

FREMONTODENDRON
Flannel bush

A GENEROUS DISPLAY OF yellow blooms cover this plant for months at a time, but flowering may be affected if the soil is too rich.

THE DARK GREEN leaves of Fremontodendron 'California Glory' provide the perfect canvas for its vibrant yellow blooms.

FEATURES

Wall shrub

This large evergreen shrub, the full name of which is *Fremontodendron californicum*, is spectacular when laden with its large bowl-shaped bright yellow flowers in summer and autumn. It grows up to 6m (20ft) tall and so needs a reasonable amount of headroom. It is a native of the USA, especially California. Unfortunately the Flannel bush can be quite a short-lived plant so it is best to propagate it to ensure you have some young replacement plants should it suddenly expire. It is a great choice for a house or other high wall and relishes a sheltered courtyard garden or other secluded area. It looks good growing with a blue-flowered ceanothus.

FREMONTODENDRON AT A GLANCE

A large vigorous shrub with shallow bowl-shaped yellow flowers over a very long period. Hardy to −5°C (23°F).

JAN	/	RECOMMENDED VARIETIES
FEB	/	*Fremontodendron* 'California
MAR	/	Glory', deep yellow flowers.
APR	planting ✍	
MAY	planting ✍	
JUN	flowering ❀	
JULY	flowering ❀	
AUG	flowering ❀	
SEP	flowering ❀	
OCT	flowering ❀	
NOV	/	
DEC	/	

CONDITIONS

Aspect   Grow against a warm sunny wall. Needs to be well sheltered from wind.

Site   Can be grown in a wide range of well-drained soils, from dry to moist, but prefers alkaline or neutral conditions. Ideally suited to poor soils.

GROWING METHOD

Propagation   Sow seeds in spring and germinate at 15–20°C (59–68°F). Take semi-ripe cuttings in late summer and root in a heated propagating case. Hardwood cuttings in late autumn or winter are easier. Root them in a cool glasshouse.

Watering   This plant takes quite dry conditions, so it is not necessary to water unless the soil becomes excessively dry.

Feeding   Give an annual application of slow-release organic fertilizer in the spring.

Problems   Not generally troubled by pests or diseases.

FLOWERING/FOLIAGE

Flowers   It is grown for its flamboyant yellow flowers produced over a very long period.

Foliage   Dark green lobed leaves. Shoots hairy and covered in scales.

PRUNING

Requirements   Minimal pruning in midsummer after the first flowers. Wear goggles: the mealy coating on the shoots and leaves can irritate the eyes.

HEBE HULKEANA
New Zealand lilac

THIS YOUNG Hebe hulkeana *needs careful training to contain its loose growth habit. It tolerates some shade, but does best in full sun.*

SHAPELY LEAVES ARE a key attraction of the hebes, and many have subtle distinguishing features, such as the thin red edging here.

FEATURES

Wall shrub

This is an evergreen shrub from New Zealand, with a slender, loose, sprawling habit of growth. It is best grown by training it to a warm sunny wall, where it will benefit from the protection afforded, as it is not one of the hardiest subjects. The New Zealand lilac is a beautiful shrub, though, and well worth growing for its spring and summer display of lavender-blue flowers. As a free-standing shrub it grows to about 1m (3ft) high, but will grow taller against a wall, up to 1.8m (6ft). For those who live in areas subject to very hard winters, this hebe can be grown in a cool conservatory. It will particularly enjoy and thrive in mild seaside gardens. The *Hebe* genus as a whole is valued by gardeners for its versatility, fine flowers and neat foliage.

HEBE HULKEANA AT A GLANCE

A loose, slender evergreen shrub with heads of lavender-blue flowers. Hardy to −5°C (23°F).

		COMPANION PLANTS
JAN	/	Associates well with early-flowering climbing roses with pink or red flowers
FEB	/	
MAR	/	
APR	planting ✍	
MAY	flowering ❀	
JUN	flowering ❀	
JULY	/	
AUG	/	
SEP	/	
OCT	/	
NOV	/	
DEC	/	

CONDITIONS

Aspect Will grow in sun or partial shade, but needs to be well protected from cold drying winds.

Site This plant requires well-drained yet moisture-retentive soil, ranging from alkaline to neutral and low to moderate fertility.

GROWING METHOD

Propagation Take softwood cuttings in spring or early summer, or semi-ripe cuttings in summer. It is best to have some young plants in reserve to replace the main plant if it is killed off by hard frosts.

Watering Do not let the plant dry out. Water if the soil starts to become dry in summer.

Feeding Once a year, in spring, apply a slow-release organic fertilize, such as blood, fish and bone.

Problems These plants may be attacked by aphids in spring or summer.

FLOWERING/FOLIAGE

Flowers This shrub is grown primarily for its flowers, which are produced in decorative trusses on the ends of the shoots.

Foliage The shiny evergreen elliptic leaves with red edges are attractive.

PRUNING

Requirements No regular pruning needed. Spread out and train young stems to their supports. Cut back any frost-damaged or dead growth in spring. Remove dead flower heads.

HEDERA
Ivy

FOR A *particularly lush and wild look to a corner of the garden, Ivy will quickly cover the trunk of a mature tree with dense foliage.*

HEDERA COLCHICA *boasts probably the largest leaves of all ivies, with a soft, leathery texture and bright young growth.*

FEATURES

Self clinging climber

Most people are familiar with the native English or Common ivy, *Hedera helix*, with its deep green, lobed leaves that cover the ground in shady places, such as woods, under hedgerows and on banks. But it is not always realized that this plant has produced many cultivars that are much more attractive than the wild plant. They vary greatly in the form and size of leaf, as well as in the colour of the foliage, which comes in many shades of green, or sometimes splashed, spotted or edged with gold, cream or white.

There are so many excellent cultivars for the garden that it is difficult to make a choice, but the following can be recommended: 'Adam', variegated cream-white, height 5m (15ft); 'Buttercup', bright yellow, 2m (6ft); 'Glacier', grey and cream, 2m (6ft); 'Goldheart' (syn. 'Oro di Bogliasco'), bright yellow centre, 8m (25ft); 'Pedata', green bird's foot shaped leaves, 4m (12ft); and 'Tricolor', grey-green,

cream and pink variegation, 1.5m (5ft).

Then there are larger-leaved ivies that are also well worth growing, but some are not quite so hardy as the English ivy. The Canary Island ivy, *H. canariensis*, a native of North Africa, has much larger leaves than English ivy. They are three-lobed, bright green and shiny. There are several good cultivars that are also worth growing, including 'Gloire de Marengo' with white and green variegated leaves, and 'Ravensholst' with very deep green leaves. The Canary Island ivy is moderately vigorous in habit and can reach a height of 4m (12ft). It is best grown in a sheltered position.

Also with very large leaves is the Persian ivy, *H. colchica*, a native of Iran and the Caucasus. It is a hardy plant and a very vigorous grower, reaching 10m (30ft) in height. Its leaves are not lobed, but they are leathery in texture and deep green. There are numerous cultivars of this species including 'Dentata' with bright green leaves; the white and grey variegated 'Dentata Variegata'; and 'Sulphur Heart', which is variegated with creamy yellow.

In general ivy is very long lived, rather vigorous and tolerant of poor conditions, including polluted air. It is a self-clinging climber, producing aerial roots on its stems, so it is able to fix itself to smooth surfaces, such as walls and fences. It is probably best not to grow ivy on the walls of the house, as it will be difficult to remove should any maintenance work become necessary. Ivy will readily climb mature trees and at the other extreme makes superb ground cover in shrub borders, woodland gardens and on shady banks. For quickly covering an unsightly outbuilding, ivy is often the first choice. If that were not enough, ivy can also be grown in patio tubs and trained into standards. The various cultivars of the small-leaved *H. helix* are particularly good for this purpose.

HEDERA AT A GLANCE

Self-clinging evergreen climbers whose leaves vary in shape, size and colour. Hardy to −15°C (5°F); *H. canariensis* is hardy to −5°C (23°F).

JAN	foliage	
FEB	foliage	
MAR	planting	
APR	planting	
MAY	foliage	
JUN	foliage	
JULY	foliage	
AUG	foliage	
SEP	foliage	
OCT	foliage	
NOV	foliage	
DEC	foliage	

COMPANION PLANTS
As ground cover, grow ivies under trees and shrubs. As climbers on walls ivies look good with *Jasminum nudiflorum* for winter effect.

IVY RESPONDS *well to clipping and can be trained into a multitude of shapes. Here it has been trained to encircle a small pond.*

A NEAT LAYER *of ivy tops this decorative fence. Regular trimming is needed during the growing season to maintain the shape.*

A CARPET *of* H. canariensis *has formed at the base of this tree. The vigorous plants are also beginning to make their way up the trunk.*

CONDITIONS

Aspect Ivies will grow in sun or shade. The green-leaved kinds take deeper shade than the coloured or variegated cultivars, the latter needing brighter light to produce best colour.

Site Ivies will grow in a wide range of soils, both moist and dry, poor and fertile. However, the best conditions are moisture-retentive yet well-drained soil of moderate fertility and containing plenty of humus. Alkaline soils are preferred but ivies will also grow well enough in acid or lime-free soils.

GROWING METHOD

Propagation Take softwood leaf-bud cuttings in spring or summer. Ivies grown as ground cover will self-layer, so dig up rooted stems as required. If you are propagating ivies for use as ground cover, do not support the young plants with canes, but simply allow them to trail. Young plants intended for climbing will need the support of a cane to start with.

Watering Ivies are tolerant of dry conditions, but for best growth water them generously if the soil starts to dry out in summer.

Feeding Apply a slow-release organic fertilizer in the spring, such as blood, fish and bone.

Problems Can be infested with aphids or scale insects.

FLOWERING/FOLIAGE

Flowers Insignificant. Ivies are grown for their foliage.

Foliage Evergreen, plain green or variegated.

PRUNING

Requirements Ivies growing on walls or fences can be trimmed with shears in early spring to prevent them becoming heavy, with the possibility of them falling away from their support. Neglected ivies will even take hard trimming, right back to the main framework of stems.

HOLBOELLIA LATIFOLIA
Holboellia

THE GLOSSY eye-shaped leaves of Holboellia latifolia are a principal attraction of this appealing climber.

HANGING IN GENTLE cascades from a house wall, H. latifolia creates a verdure of pleasant sun-catching foliage.

FEATURES

Twiner

This unusual spring-flowering evergreen climber is originally a native of Asia, and is particularly at home in the foothills of the Himalaya mountain range. It is not one of the hardiest climbers but it will thrive in gardens in the milder parts of the country if it is provided with a warm and sheltered situation. Holboellia is grown just as much for its attractive foliage as for its decorative purple female flowers. When situated in suitable conditions it is a vigorous climber, growing up to 5m (15ft) tall. It is suitable for growing on a pergola, arbour or arch, or for growing up a mature tree. A high wall makes another suitable support, as does a trellis screen.

HOLBOELLIA AT A GLANCE

Spring-flowering evergreen climber with purple flowers and handsome deep green foliage. Hardy to –5°C (23°F).

JAN	foliage 🌱	COMPANION PLANTS
FEB	foliage 🌱	Makes a good partner for spring-flowering clematis.
MAR	planting 🌿	
APR	flowering ❀	
MAY	flowering ❀	
JUN	foliage 🌱	
JULY	foliage 🌱	
SEP	foliage 🌱	
OCT	foliage 🌱	
NOV	foliage 🌱	
DEC	foliage 🌱	

CONDITIONS

Aspect Grows in full sun or partial shade. Must provide shelter from wind, which could result in damage to the plant.

Site Any well-drained yet moisture-retentive soil that contains plenty of humus.

GROWING METHOD

Propagation Sow seeds in the spring and germinate in a temperature of 16°C (61°F). Take semi-ripe cuttings in late summer. Layer stems in spring.

Watering If the soil starts to become excessively dry in summer, water the plant well.

Feeding In the spring each year apply a slow-release organic fertilizer, such as blood, fish and bone.

Problems Not troubled by pests or diseases.

FLOWERING/FOLIAGE

Flowers Male flowers are green-white, female flowers are purple. Both are borne on the same plant. Long red or purple fruits may follow, but cannot be guaranteed.

Foliage Deep green, consisting of elliptical leaflets.

PRUNING

Requirements Needs no regular pruning but you can, if desired, shorten side shoots to six buds in summer, as these tend to be vigorous and spread outwards. Or just trim the plant in summer to fit allotted space.

HUMULUS LUPULUS
Golden hop

THE COLOURING OF Humulus lupus *'Aureus'* is light but vibrant, making it ideal for brightening up a dull wall in summer.

The large leaves have three very distinctive lobes. The plant is herbaceous, dying down to the ground for the winter.

FEATURES

Twiner

Humulus lupulus 'Aureus' is a herbaceous climber that dies down to the ground for the winter. The large, lobed, golden yellow leaves provide a brilliant splash of colour in the summer garden. Of vigorous habit, it can grow up to 6m (20ft) tall. The Golden hop is suitable for a pergola, arch, arbour, trellis screen, or a tall obelisk in a mixed or shrub border, and it can also be grown in a large tub on a patio. Also let it twine through a large mature shrub, but bear in mind then that it will not be easy to prune. *Humulus lupulus* 'Aureus' can also be grown into hedges, to liven up dull textures in the garden. *H. l.* 'Taff's Variegated' has variegated foliage.

HUMULUS LUPULUS AT A GLANCE

A herbaceous climber with large golden leaves. This plant is hardy to temperatures of −15°C (5°F).

JAN	/	**COMPANION PLANTS**
FEB	planting 🖐	Try growing it with a
MAR	planting 🖐	clematis that needs annual
APR	planting 🖐	hard pruning such as the
MAY	foliage 🍂	purple 'Jackmanii'. Allow
JUN	foliage 🍂	the two to intertwine.
JULY	foliage 🍂	
AUG	foliage 🍂	
SEP	foliage 🍂	
OCT	foliage 🍂	
NOV	/	
DEC	/	

CONDITIONS

Aspect The Golden hop needs a sunny position for best leaf colour.

Site It grows well in any reasonably fertile, well-drained yet moisture-retentive soil that contains plenty of humus.

GROWING METHOD

Propagation The easiest method of propagating this climber is to carry out serpentine layering in the spring. The stems should be well rooted by the autumn when they can be lifted and planted elsewhere.

Watering Keep the plant well-watered during dry spells in the summer.

Feeding Apply a slow-release organic fertilizer in the spring each year, such as blood, fish and bone.

Problems Not generally troubled by pests or diseases.

FLOWERING/FOLIAGE

Flowers Although hops do flower, the blooms are not particularly showy. This is essentially valued as a foliage climber.

Foliage Large lobed leaves make a brilliant splash of colour in the summer. They are certainly among the most colourful of all climbers.

PRUNING

Requirements Cut the dead stems down to the ground in early spring.

HYDRANGEA ANOMALA
Climbing hydrangea

THIS HEALTHY climbing hydrangea is just coming into bloom and will soon produce an abundance of flowers for the summer.

A TREE serves as support for a climbing hydrangea, which will no doubt reach the treetop eventually. It will not need pruning here.

FEATURES

Self-clinging climber

Climbing by means of aerial roots, *Hydrangea anomala* ssp. *petiolaris* is a deciduous plant that can cover an enormous expanse of wall and has been known to climb buildings at least 15m (50ft) high. So it is not the right choice for a small area of wall. It is, however, ideal for growing up large mature trees. If you are really stuck for space, try training it as a standard in a tub. It makes good ground cover, particularly where large areas need to be carpeted. A long-lived climber, it produces creamy white 'lace-cap' flowers in summer. Being a native of Japan, Sakhalin, Korea and Taiwan, it is very hardy.

HYDRANGEA AT A GLANCE

Very vigorous climber with abundant lush foliage and creamy white lacecap flowers. Hardy to −15°C (5°F).

JAN	/	COMPANION PLANTS
FEB	planting 🌱	Due to its vigour, this plant
MAR	planting 🌱	is best grown on its own,
APR	planting 🌱	although it would look good
MAY	/	with a vigorous red rambler
JUN	flowering ✿	rose as a partner.
JULY	flowering ✿	
AUG	flowering ✿	
SEP	/	
OCT	/	
NOV	/	
DEC	/	

CONDITIONS

Aspect	Suitable for shade or semi-shade.
Site	It likes moist soil that is rich in humus and of moderate fertility. It must be well drained.

GROWING METHOD

Propagation	Best propagated by serpentine layering in the spring. The stems take about a year to form a good root system.
Watering	Water well during prolonged dry periods.
Feeding	Apply slow-release organic fertilizer in spring.
Problems	Prone to attacks by aphids and scale insects. Powdery mildew may appear on the leaves.

FLOWERING/FOLIAGE

Flowers	Grown primarily for its flowers. Each head contains both fertile and sterile flowers.
Foliage	Large heart-shaped leaves are deep green but turn yellow in the autumn before they fall.

PRUNING

Requirements The climbing hydrangea needs minimal pruning. Cut back long shoots after flowering if they outgrow their allotted space. Plants produce most flowers at the top so try not to prune back the upper growth. Old plants can be renovated by hard pruning in early spring, to leave only the main stems. Spread this over several years to avoid losing too much flower.

JASMINUM
Jasmine

THE GLOSSY lance-shaped leaves of jasmine are decorative enough to earn it a place in the garden even if it didn't produce its flowers.

TREASURED for their subtle fragrance, the flowers of Jasminum officinale *also make a delightful display in summer and autumn.*

FEATURES

Scramblers
twiners

These deciduous and evergreen climbers are among the most popular of all, many being valued for their sweetly fragrant flowers. Due to their informal habit they are great favourites for cottage and country gardens, where they combine well with old-fashioned flowers. Try grouping them with old-fashioned roses, for instance, and shrubs such as philadelphus (Mock orange), which is also highly scented. But the versatile jasmines can be used in any type of garden. They can be grown up and over various kinds of support. Use them to cover walls, fences, trellis screens, pergolas, arches and arbours. They can even be trained up large mature trees. Large mature shrubs might also make good hosts, but then pruning of the jasmines becomes more difficult.

JASMINUM AT A GLANCE

Scrambling or twining climbers. The species mentioned in the main text are hardy to –5°C (23°F), *J. nudiflorum* is hardy to –15°C (5°F).

JAN	flowering
FEB	flowering
MAR	planting
APR	planting
MAY	flowering
JUN	flowering
JULY	flowering
AUG	flowering
SEP	flowering
OCT	/
NOV	/
DEC	flowering

COMPANION PLANTS
Jasmines look lovely intertwining with climbing or rambler roses. Ivy is a good companion for the winter jasmine.

There are many species of jasmine but some are too tender to be grown out of doors in cold climates. These are best grown in a cool conservatory. However, there are still many good species suitable for growing in gardens, including *Jasminum beesianum*, a Chinese twiner that is evergreen in milder gardens but deciduous in colder areas. The flowers, produced in the first half of the summer, are fragrant and red-pink in colour. It grows to a height of 5m (15ft) so would be suitable for training on a wall of the house.

Jasminum humile 'Revolutum' (Yellow jasmine), is of garden origin, but the species is a native of China, Afghanistan and the Himalayas. This semi-evergreen scrambler has bright yellow scented flowers in late spring and early summer and reaches a height of at least 2.5m (8ft). Again this is another suitable species for the walls of the house.

The ever-popular Winter jasmine, *J. nudiflorum*, is a scrambling, deciduous, Chinese shrub that is ideally suited to training to a wall. The green stems and shoots carry bright yellow flowers in winter and into spring. Height 3m (10ft). It can also be used as ground cover to clothe a bank.

Jasminum officinale (Common jasmine), a twining, deciduous climber from China and the Himalayas, can grow up to 12m (40ft) in height, but may be kept shorter by pruning. It is an extremely popular species and an essential choice for cottage gardens. Sweetly scented white flowers appear in summer and autumn. There are several good cultivars and forms including *J. o.* f. *affine* whose white flowers are tinted with pink; 'Aureum' with yellow-variegated leaves; and 'Argenteovariegatum' with white-edged leaves.

JASMINE MAKES a perfect plant to drape over various garden structures, and here forms a scented canopy over an arbour.

MASSES OF FLOWERS adorn Jasminum nudiflorum *from late autumn to early spring, providing a wall of colour.*

CONDITIONS

Aspect Ideally jasmines should be grown in full sun, where they flower most freely, but partial shade is acceptable. The Winter jasmine, especially, is suitable for partial shade.

Site Jasmines are highly adaptable plants and will grow in any well-drained and reasonably fertile soil. The soil should be capable of retaining moisture during dry weather – so add bulky organic matter before planting.

GROWING METHOD

Propagation The easiest way to propagate jasmines is to carry out serpentine layering in the spring. Alternatively take semi-ripe cuttings in summer. However, hardwood cuttings in winter are better for *J. nudiflorum* and *J. officinale*, rooting them in a cold frame or in a cool glasshouse.

Watering It is important not to allow jasmines to suffer from extended lack of moisture, try to keep the plants well watered during any prolonged dry spells if necessary.

Feeding Apply a slow-release fertilizer annually in the spring just as growth is starting. Blood, fish and bone is a good organic choice.

Problems Jasmines may be attacked by aphids, but these pests are easily controlled by spraying with a suitable insecticide.

FLOWERING/FOLIAGE

Flowers Jasmines are grown primarily for their flowers, which are often highly fragrant.

Foliage Many jasmines have pinnate foliage. It may be evergreen or deciduous, depending on species and/or climate.

PRUNING

Requirements Jasmines vary in their pruning requirements according to species. *Jasminum humile* 'Revolutum' needs thinning out regularly to prevent congested growth. When flowering is over, cut out completely no more than two of the oldest stems. Neglected and overgrown plants can be renovated by cutting them back hard in early spring.

Jasminum nudiflorum requires annual pruning. This should take place as soon as flowering is over. Carry out spur pruning by cutting back the old flowered shoots to within two or three pairs of buds of the main framework of the plant.

For established plants of *J. officinale* and *J. beesianum* thin out congested growth as soon as flowering is over by cutting back the flowered shoots. If necessary neglected plants can be hard pruned by cutting back old stems to within 90cm (3ft) of the ground in late winter or early spring.

LONICERA
Honeysuckle

TOLERANT OF PARTIAL shade, Lonicera japonica *'Halliana' is also fast-growing and makes an ideal cover for pergolas.*

THE FLUTED BLOOMS of Lonicera sempervirens *hang in attractive bunches that add to their visual impact.*

FEATURES

Twiners

Honeysuckles are widely grown climbers, ranking in popularity with clematis and jasmines. Like the latter, many have highly fragrant flowers and are valued for this alone, but the blooms also make a colourful display in the summer.

They have a very informal habit of growth, making them ideally suited to cottage and country gardens, where they could be grown with old-fashioned flowers and other plants, such as old roses. Try growing them with climbing roses and let them intertwine for some really stunning effects, although bear in mind that pruning of both may then be more difficult. Owners of more modern gardens should also consider growing honeysuckles as they will not look out of place.

Honeysuckles can be grown up a variety of supports, including walls, fences, pergolas, arbours, arches, obelisks in a shrub border, and large mature trees. They look particularly at home in a woodland garden, as they often grow in woodland conditions in the wild. The Common honeysuckle or Woodbine, *Lonicera periclymenum* and its cultivars, makes good ground cover in shrub borders and woodland gardens. Some species can be grown in tubs and trained as standards, including *L. japonica* 'Halliana' (Japanese honeysuckle) and *L. periclymenum* cultivars.

There are many species and cultivars to choose from but the following are probably among the best loved. *Lonicera* x *brownii* 'Fuchsioides' (Scarlet trumpet honeysuckle), has clusters of slightly fragrant, tubular, orange-scarlet flowers in summer. A twiner of garden origin, it is deciduous or, in some climates, evergreen, and can attain a height of 4m (12ft).

Lonicera caprifolium, (Italian honeysuckle), a native of Europe and western Asia, is a deciduous twiner producing, in summer, clusters of highly fragrant, tubular, cream or yellow flowers flushed with pink. It can grow to a height of 6m (20ft).

The extremely vigorous *L. japonica* 'Halliana' (Japanese honeysuckle), is a semi-evergreen or evergreen twiner with white tubular flowers which turn yellow as they age. The blooms are highly fragrant and the flowering period is from spring to the end of summer. It grows to a height of 10m (30ft). The species is a native of eastern Asia.

The Common honeysuckle, also known as Woodbine, *L. periclymenum*, is a native of Britain where it scrambles over hedgerows.

LONICERA AT A GLANCE

Vigorous twiners with tubular flowers in summer. Hardy to temperatures of up to −15°C (5°F).

JAN	/	
FEB	planting ✆	**COMPANION PLANTS**
MAR	planting ✆	Honeysuckles look good
APR	planting ✆	accompanied by climbing
MAY	flowering ✿	or rambler roses.
JUN	flowering ✿	
JULY	flowering ✿	
AUG	flowering ✿	
SEP	flowering ✿	
OCT	/	
NOV	/	
DEC	/	

A PROFUSION of flowers smothers this Lonicera pericylmenum 'Belgica'. The flowers fill the air with their powerful fragrance.

THE DELICATE TUBULAR flowers of Lonicera pericylmenum 'Belgica' are prized for their perfume and distinctive appearance.

It is a very vigorous twiner that produces fragrant flowers from mid- to late summer. The species is not generally grown in gardens, most gardeners preferring to use its cultivars. *L. p.* 'Belgica' is popularly known as the Early Dutch honeysuckle and has white blooms that age to yellow. These are flushed with red on the outside. *L. p.* 'Serotina' is the Late Dutch honeysuckle with cream flowers that are flushed with reddish-purple on the outside. Both of these decorative cultivars can grow up to 6m (20ft) tall.

Hailing from the USA, *Lonicera sempervirens*, known as Trumpet honeysuckle, is an evergreen or deciduous twiner with tubular flowers that are reddish orange on the outside but yellow-orange within. The flowers are produced throughout summer and into autumn. It reaches up to 4m (12ft) in height.

CONDITIONS

Aspect   All species and their cultivars will grow in full sun or partial shade.

Site   Honeysuckles are very adaptable and will grow in any well-drained but moisture-retentive, humus-rich soil of reasonable fertility.

GROWING METHOD

Propagation   The easiest method of propagation is to carry out serpentine layering in the spring. Alternatively take softwood or semi-ripe cuttings in spring and summer. Sow seeds in autumn and stratify over winter.

Watering   Do not let honeysuckles suffer from prolonged lack of moisture. Water the plants thoroughly if the soil starts to dry out during long dry periods in the summer.

Feeding   Apply a slow-release fertilizer, such as the organic blood, fish and bone, in the spring.

Problems   Plants may become infested with aphids during the summer.

FLOWERING/FOLIAGE

Flowers   Honeysuckles are grown primarily for their flowers, and the scented kinds are most popular.

Foliage   Evergreen or deciduous, the leaves being arranged in opposite pairs.

PRUNING

Requirements   The congested growth of *Lonicera japonica* can be thinned out in early spring. Prune back any very long shoots. If renovation is needed, cut back the entire plant to within 90cm (3ft) of the ground in late winter or early spring. With the species *L. periclymenum*, *L. x brownii*, *L. caprifolium* and *L. sempervirens*, you can either allow them to grow at will or reduce the flowered shoots by one-third in early spring to restrict the size of the plant. Shears may be used to trim the entire plant. Renovation pruning is the same as for *L. japonica*.

MUEHLENBECKIA
Wire vine

A CLOSE-UP OF Muehlenbeckia complexa's foliage showing the intricate pattern created by the tiny leaves and winding stems.

THE SMALL LEAVES of M. complexa create a cloudlike effect, and make it an exceptional climber for masking objects.

FEATURES

Twiner

Muehlenbeckia complexa (Wire vine) is a semi-deciduous climber from New Zealand, not often seen in gardens. Yet it is easily grown and has a most unusual habit of growth. It forms a dense tangle of very thin, wiry stems and is capable of growing up to 3m (10ft) tall when trained vertically. The Wire vine, or wire-netting plant as it is sometimes called, has tiny rounded leaves with attractive purple or silvery undersides. It is a good climber for low structures and excellent for covering a chain-link fence or trellis screen. It makes unusual ground cover in a shrub border and is ideal for covering a bank.

MUEHLENBECKIA AT A GLANCE

Twiner producing a mass of wire-like stems bearing tiny rounded leaves. Hardy to –5°C (23°F).

JAN	/	COMPANION PLANTS
FEB	/	Makes a good background
MAR	/	for many plants, particularly
APR	planting 🌱	other New Zealand natives
MAY	planting 🌱	like phormiums
JUN	foliage 🍂	
JULY	foliage 🍂	
AUG	foliage 🍂	
SEP	foliage 🍂	
OCT	/	
NOV	/	
DEC	/	

CONDITIONS

Aspect	It likes a position in full sun but appreciates shade during the hottest part of the day. Provide shelter from cold winds
Site	This climber grows in any well-drained yet moisture-retentive soil of reasonable fertility.

GROWING METHOD

Propagation	Sow seeds as soon as collected and germinate them in a temperature of 19–24°C (66–75°F).
Watering	Apply water to the plant if the soil starts to become excessively dry in summer.
Feeding	Apply a slow-release organic fertilizer, such as blood, fish and bone, in the spring.
Problems	The wire vine is not generally troubled by pests or diseases.

FLOWERING/FOLIAGE

Flowers	In summer tiny green-white flowers appear but they are insignificant – this plant is grown primarily for its overall habit of growth.
Foliage	A semi-deciduous climber with very small rounded leaves.

PRUNING

Requirements	No regular pruning needed. Trim lightly if necessary to restrict the overall size of the plant. Do not prune too hard or you will risk spoiling the habit of the plant.

PARTHENOCISSUS
Boston ivy and Virginia creeper

THESE BOSTON IVY LEAVES look shiny and rather like grape leaves. The autumn tones can be quite brilliant.

THE WALLS and entrance of this house are completely blanketed in Boston ivy. In time, a plant can grow to cover a very large area.

FEATURES

Tendril climbers

The parthenocissus are extremely vigorous deciduous climbers that provide some of the most brilliant autumn leaf colour of any plant. *Parthenocissus tricuspidata*, Boston ivy, a native of Japan, China and Korea, is a vigorous and long-lived climber, often used to cover large walls or fences. It is capable of reaching a height of 20m (70ft), and its vigour makes it unsuitable for small gardens. The large leaves are bright, shiny green and lobed. Boston ivy is deciduous, and provides a brilliant display of autumn colour – generally bright red. It is classed as a tendril climber but is self-clinging by means of adhesive suckers. The cultivar 'Lowii' is smaller growing and has smaller leaves, while the foliage of 'Veitchii' turns deep reddish purple in the autumn.

Parthenocissus henryana (Chinese Virginia creeper) has the same climbing habit as the Boston ivy but is much less vigorous. Even so it can attain a height of 10m (30ft). It has deep green hand-shaped leaves with white veins. It also provides a brilliant red autumn display.

Parthenocissus quinquefolia is the true Virginia creeper, a native of eastern North America. It is vigorous, capable of climbing a wall up to 15m (50ft) high to which it will cling tenaciously with its sucker pads. The leaves are hand-shaped and medium green, not the most attractive – until that is, in autumn, when they turn brilliant red and equal any pyrotechnic display.

Although in general parthenocissus are too large for ordinary gardens when grown as climbers, they are much easier to control as ground cover plants. They are particularly suitable for clothing banks. Plant them at the top and they will soon cascade down the bank, creating the effect of molten lava in the autumn. These climbers are ideal for growing up large mature trees. Dark green conifers make superb hosts because the parthenocissus' vivid autumnal display really shows up well. Boston ivy and Virginia creepers will quickly cover large, unsightly outbuildings. It is not recommended that parthenocissus are grown on the house walls, unless the house is exceedingly large, as they will soon grow up and over the roof and block gutters and obscure windows. They need a lot of trimming to keep them within bounds. Also it will be impossible to remove the stems without causing them damage, should this be necessary for house maintenance. Admittedly, though, parthenocissus are often seen growing on 'ordinary' houses.

PARTHENOCISSUS AT A GLANCE

Extremely vigorous tendril climbers with lobed leaves that take on brilliant tints in autumn. Hardy to –15°C (5°F).

JAN	/	**COMPANION PLANTS**
FEB	planting 🌱	Due to size and vigour,
MAR	planting 🌱	companion plants are not
APR	planting 🌱	applicable. However, tall
MAY	/	mature conifers will make
JUN	/	good hosts.
JULY	/	
AUG	/	
SEP	foliage 🍂	
OCT	foliage 🍂	
NOV	/	
DEC	/	

THE CHINESE Virginia creeper, Parthenocissus henryana, is notable for its white-veined leaves, which colour up well in autumn.

THE VIGOROUS GROWTH of P. henryana makes it capable of covering large objects, even entire houses, in just a few years.

A BLUE WOODEN clapboard fence provides a fine background for the green and white leaves of this young P. henryana.

CONDITIONS

Aspect These species will grow in sun or shade. Partial shade is the ideal for *P. henryana* as in these conditions it produces its best colour.

Site Parthenocissus will grow well in any type of soil but it should be reasonably fertile and certainly well drained.

GROWING METHOD

Propagation Take softwood or semi-ripe cuttings in spring and summer. Hardwood cuttings taken in winter and rooted in frost-free conditions are more successful. Sow seeds in autumn and stratify over winter.

Watering Parthenocissus can survive quite dry conditions once established but it pays to water them if the soil starts to become excessively dry during the summer.

Feeding Apply a slow-release fertilizer, such as the organic blood, fish and bone, in the spring.

Problems These climbers are not usually troubled by pests or diseases.

FLOWERING/FOLIAGE

Flowers Insignificant. Parthenocissus are grown primarily for their foliage.

Foliage The foliage takes on brilliant tints in autumn. In the summer the leaves create a pleasing green cover for the support.

PRUNING

Requirements No regular pruning needed. Simply trim with shears to keep the plant within its allotted space. This is best done in the early winter, but summer trimming can also be carried out if necessary. To renovate an old neglected plant, cut it down to within 90cm (3ft) of the ground in winter.

PASSIFLORA CAERULEA
Blue passion flower

THE FLOWERS of Passiflora *are famous for their intricate petals and stamens. Only* P. caerulea *is hardy enough to be grown outside.*

MILDLY FRAGRANCED and producing yellow or orange fruit in late summer and early autumn, P. caerulea *provides plenty of interest.*

FEATURES

Tendril climber

The Blue passion flower is a fast-growing climber from Brazil and Argentina with evergreen or semi-evergreen foliage. The very complex flowers, basically bowl shaped, come in a striking colour combination of white and green, zoned with blue, purple and white. This species grows to at least 10m (30ft) tall. As it is not one of the hardiest climbers available the Blue passion flower is best grown against a warm, sunny, sheltered wall. This makes it an ideal subject for a courtyard garden or any similar enclosed area. Alternatively, it could be grown on the wall of the house. It really flourishes in mild parts of the country, and in colder areas this plant will need adequate protection from cold drying winds.

PASSIFLORA AT A GLANCE

A vigorous tendril climber producing exotic-looking flowers followed by orange fruits. Hardy to −5°C (23°F).

JAN	/	RECOMMENDED VARIETIES
FEB	/	*P. c.* 'Constance Elliot' has
MAR	/	white flowers.
APR	planting 🌱	
MAY	planting 🌱	
JUN	flowering ❁	
JULY	flowering ❁	
AUG	flowering ❁	
SEP	flowering ❁	
OCT	flowering ❁	
NOV	/	
DEC	/	

CONDITIONS

Aspect Best in full sun but can also be grown in partial shade. This plant needs to be well sheltered from cold winds

Site Grows in any reasonably fertile, well-drained yet moisture-retentive soil.

GROWING METHOD

Propagation Take softwood or semi-ripe leaf-bud cuttings in spring and summer. Carry out serpentine layering in the spring. Sow seeds in spring, after soaking in hot water for 24 hours. Germinate at 18°C (64°F).

Watering If the soil starts to dry out in the summer water the plant well.

Feeding Apply a slow-release fertilizer in the spring, such as the organic blood, fish and bone.

Problems Passifloras are not usually troubled by pests and diseases out of doors.

FLOWERING/FOLIAGE

Flowers Bowl-shaped flowers over a very long period, followed by egg-shaped light orange fruits.

Foliage Dark green and deeply lobed.

PRUNING

Requirements Train a framework of permanent stems on the support and in spring just before growth starts, carry out spur pruning by cutting back flowered shoots to within two or three buds of this framework.

PERIPLOCA GRAECA
Silk vine

THE STAR-SHAPED flowers of Periploca graeca, *the Silk vine, are followed by silky seeds, hence the common name.*

THIS EXOTIC VARIETY, Periploca laevigata, *a native of north Africa and the Canary Islands, produces amazing star-shaped flowers.*

FEATURES

Twiner

This is a vigorous deciduous climber, a native of south-west Europe and south-west Asia. The Silk vine is grown primarily for its attractive-looking star-shaped flowers in the summer. Unfortunately these flowers also have a rather unpleasant fragrance. It is the most commonly grown species, of which there are about 11 altogether in the genus. Growing to a height of 9m (28ft), the Silk vine is suitable for a warm sheltered wall or close-boarded fence where it will be well protected. This plant is also suitable for a pergola or trellis screen, as long as the chosen site is well sheltered from cold and drying winds. It will make an ideal climber for a courtyard garden with its own favourable microclimate.

PERIPLOCA GRAECA AT A GLANCE

A vigorous deciduous climber with star-shaped yellow-green and purple flowers in summer. Hardy to –5°C (23°F).

JAN	/	
FEB	/	
MAR	planting 🌱	
APR	planting 🌱	
MAY	/	
JUN	/	
JULY	flowering ❁	
AUG	flowering ❁	
SEP	/	
OCT	/	
NOV	/	
DEC	/	

COMPANION PLANTS
Grow with other climbers and wall shrubs that need similar conditions, such as *Abutilon megapotamicum.*

CONDITIONS

Aspect The Silk vine requires a position in full sun that is also warm and sheltered.

Site Any soil is suitable provided it is well drained.

GROWING METHOD

Propagation Sow seeds in the spring and germinate them in a temperature of 16°C (61°F). Root semi-ripe cuttings during the summer.

Watering Do not let this climber suffer from drought. Water the plant well if the soil starts to dry out excessively.

Feeding An annual application, during the spring, of a slow-release fertilizer will keep the plant going. The organic blood, fish and bone is a suitable choice.

Problems The Silk vine is not usually troubled by any pests or diseases.

FLOWERING/FOLIAGE

Flowers Star shaped, yellow-green and purple, followed by long thin seed pods that split open to reveal silky seeds, hence the common name.

Foliage Deep green shiny leaves make a good background for the flowers.

PRUNING

Requirements In early spring simply trim if necessary to keep the plant within its allotted space. Eventually renovation pruning may be needed by thinning out the oldest stems.

PILEOSTEGIA VIBURNOIDES
Pileostegia

PILEOSTEGIA VIBURNOIDES *shows a fetching contrast between its bold leaves and its lacy puffs of cream-white flowers*

DRAMATIC FIREWORK *bursts of white, the flowers of* P. viburnoides *reveal their intricate beauty on close inspection.*

FEATURES

Self-clinging climber

This is a very vigorous, tall-growing evergreen climber that supports itself by means of aerial roots produced from the stems. It is related to the rather similar climbing hydrangea (see page 87) and to schizophragma (see page 102). Pileostegia is a native of China, Taiwan and India. This climber is grown for its flowers, which are produced in summer and autumn, and for its dense, good-looking foliage that effectively hides the support. Growing up to 6m (20ft) in height, pileostegia is suitable for growing on high walls or up large mature trees but is not a suitable subject for small gardens or where space is restricted. It is also a good shade survivor, which might make it a suitable choice for shaded areas that other climbers cannot endure.

PILEOSTEGIA AT A GLANCE

Vigorous evergreen climber with deep green foliage and cream-white flowers in late summer and autumn. Hardy to –5°C (23°F).

JAN	/	COMPANION PLANTS
FEB	/	Due to its vigour, best
MAR	planting 🖑	grown alone, but could
APR	planting 🖑	combine with a vigorous
MAY	/	rambler rose.
JUN	/	
JULY	/	
AUG	flowering ❀	
SEP	flowering ❀	
OCT	flowering ❀	
NOV	/	
DEC	/	

CONDITIONS

Aspect   Pileostegia will endure most light conditions, from full sun to full shade.

Site   This climber will grow in any reasonably rich soil provided the drainage is good.

GROWING METHOD

Propagation   Take semi-ripe cuttings in summer and ideally root them in a cold frame.

Watering   Do not let this climber dry out excessively, so water well in prolonged dry spells in summer.

Feeding   An annual feed, in spring, of slow-release fertilizer, such as the organic blood, fish and bone, is all that is required.

Problems   Pileostegia is not troubled by pests or diseases.

FLOWERING/FOLIAGE

Flowers   The heads of cream-white flowers are produced late in the summer.

Foliage   The deep green elliptical leaves have a leathery texture.

PRUNING

Requirements   Prune in early spring. Minimal pruning needed. Shorten any over-long or badly placed shoots as necessary. This climber produces most flowers at the top so do not prune to reduce height. Hard renovation pruning is acceptable if necessary – simply leave a main framework of stems. Ideally spread this type of pruning over several years to prevent too much loss of flower following pruning.

ROSA
Rose species and hybrids

ROSA 'ALBERTINE' is a beautiful, heavily scented rambler rose, shown in this garden in its full glory. Although it produces only one long blooming each year, its lovely salmon-pink colour and scent are well worth the wait. It is one of the most popular rambler roses.

FEATURES

Scramblers

The climbing roses rank among the most popular of all climbing plants. There are climbing roses suitable for walls and fences of all sizes, and vigorous ramblers and climbers that can be allowed to grow up through large mature trees and evergreen conifers. Many climbers and ramblers are ideal for pergolas, arches, arbours and obelisks.

Modern hybrid climbers such as 'Alchemist' are the most popular. They are recurrent flowering, producing several flushes of flowers in summer, and there is a large range to choose from in a wide selection of colours. Older cultivars may have only one flush of blooms.

Ramblers, both species and cultivars, are generally more vigorous than modern hybrid climbers and need plenty of space. Many have only one main flush of flowers in the summer, such as the popular old 'Albertine' and 'Wedding Day'.

Species roses are also well worth considering, including *Rosa banksiae*, the double white Banksian rose. This climber has double, sweetly scented, white flowers in late spring and is one of the earliest roses to flower. Also recommended is the yellow Banksian rose, *R. b.* 'Lutea', with double yellow flowers. The species itself is very tall, up to 12m (40ft), but the yellow cultivar is much shorter, about 6m (20ft). The Banksian roses are hardy to –5°C (23°F) and are best grown on a warm sunny sheltered wall or fence.

CONDITIONS

Aspect   Full sun is required for best flowering.
Site   Roses like a fertile, deep, moisture-retentive, yet well-drained soil. Dig in plenty of bulky organic matter before planting to provide humus, which helps to retain moisture during dry periods. Keep roses well mulched with bulky organic matter.

GROWING METHOD

Propagation   It is not really feasible for home gardeners to propagate many of the climbing roses. Commercially they are propagated by budding onto suitable rootstocks. You could try ramblers and species roses from hardwood cuttings in winter. Root them in a cold frame.
Watering   Keep roses well watered if the soil dries. They dislike very dry or drought conditions.

Feeding	You could use a proprietary rose fertilizer. Alternatively apply blood, fish and bone fertilizer. Apply in the spring as growth is starting, and after the first flush of flowers.
Problems	Roses have more than their fair share of problems: aphids, rose black spot, rose powdery mildew and rose rust, to name some of the most troublesome. Wherever possible buy disease-resistant roses. Carry out preventative spraying to control diseases, starting as soon as new foliage appears. Use a combined rose spray.

FLOWERING/FOLIAGE

Flowers	May be single, semi-double, or fully double, fragrant or without scent. Flowering may be a single flush in the summer, or repeat-flowering throughout summer.
Foliage	The leaves are made up of leaflets in varying shades of green, often shiny, but generally not particularly attractive.

PRUNING

Requirements Roses flower on current or previous year's shoots, so prune annually. Wherever possible train stems horizontally as they then produce better distributed flowers, instead of blooming only at the top. Of course, this method of training is not possible when growing on pergola pillars and obelisks. There are hybrid climbing roses that are suitable for these types of supports, or spiral training could be used to give you blooms all the way up the support.

Ramblers flower best on stems produced in the previous year, but will also flower on older ones. Prune after flowering by cutting out some of the oldest flowered stems to ground level. Then space out and tie in the remaining stems.

For modern hybrid climbers train a main framework of stems to the support. This produces side shoots that in turn produce flowers. Prune in late winter or early spring by cutting back side shoots to two or three buds from the main stems. Cut back the oldest stems once they start producing fewer flowers.

R. 'WEDDING DAY', a lovely single white rambler rose, bears a great profusion of blooms. Here it has a sturdy metal frame for support.

WELL-SPACED STEMS encourage the best flowering and allow all flowers to be seen. This peachy-apricot climbing rose is R. 'Alchemist'.

THE WEIGHT of growth from this prolific pink-flowering climbing rose may require an extra cross-bar support for the pergola.

ROSA AT A GLANCE

Summer-flowering scramblers, with flowers in a wide range of colours, many being fragrant. Most roses are hardy to −15°C (5°F).

JAN	planting 🌿	
FEB	planting 🌿	**COMPANION PLANTS**
MAR	planting 🌿	Summer-flowering clematis
APR	planting 🌿	are particularly good
MAY	flowering ✽	companions. You can allow
JUN	flowering ✽	the two to intertwine.
JULY	flowering ✽	
AUG	flowering ✽	
SEP	flowering ✽	
OCT	planting 🌿	
NOV	planting 🌿	
DEC	planting 🌿	

RUBUS HENRYI
Rubus

THE DISTINCTIVE three-fingered leaves of Rubus henryi *var.* bambusarum *are joined by pink flowers in early summer.*

MANY OF the decorative members of the Rubus *genus are grown for their glossy and pleasantly-shaped leaves.*

FEATURES

Scrambler

The genus *Rubus* is huge, containing over 250 species, some of which are well-known edible fruits such as blackberries and raspberries. There are also numerous ornamental species and one of the most decorative is *R. henryi* var. *bambusarum*. This handsome evergreen climber from China has long spiny stems with white hairs. It is grown for these attractive stems, as well as for the foliage and summer flowers. It is a vigorous plant, growing 6m (20ft) tall, and is a good subject for a shrub border or woodland garden. In these situations it can be grown either as a climber, perhaps over a large shrub, up a mature tree, or on an obelisk, or as a groundcover plant.

RUBUS HENRYI AT A GLANCE

R.h. var. *bambusarum* is a handsome blackberry relation with spiny stems and pink summer flowers. Hardy to –15°C (5°F).

JAN	/	COMPANION PLANTS
FEB	planting 🌿	This climber looks good
MAR	planting 🌿	with shrubs, particularly
APR	planting 🌿	woodland-garden kinds.
MAY	/	
JUN	flowering ✿	
JULY	flowering ✿	
AUG	flowering ✿	
SEP	/	
OCT	/	
NOV	/	
DEC	/	

CONDITIONS

Aspect Suitable for sun or partial shade.
Site *R. h.* var. *bambusarum* will grow in any soil that is well drained and reasonably fertile.

GROWING METHOD

Propagation Take semi-ripe cuttings in summer. You can also use semi-ripe leaf-bud cuttings. Layer stems in the spring. Groundcover plants may self-layer.
Watering It likes moist conditions so do not allow the plant to dry out during prolonged dry spells in summer.
Feeding Apply a slow-release fertilizer in the spring, such as the organic blood, fish and bone.
Problems Not generally troubled by pests or diseases.

FLOWERING/FOLIAGE

Flowers Clusters of small bowl-shaped pink flowers are followed by shiny black berries.
Foliage The shiny deep green three-lobed leaves with white undersides are very attractive.

PRUNING

Requirements Pruning aims to ensure plenty of new stems, so in late winter or early spring each year cut some of the stems that produced flowers the previous year down to ground level. New shoots will then appear from the base of the plant in the spring.

SCHISANDRA CHINENSIS
Schisandra

THE LUSH *deciduous foliage of the Asian climber* Schisandra chinensis *contrasts well with a red brick wall.*

NESTLING AMID *the leaves of a female* S. chinensis, *berries are just beginning to blush a light shade of red.*

FEATURES

Twiner

The genus contains about two dozen species, some of which are evergreen, others being deciduous. *Schisandra chinensis* is one of the best known and most widely grown. It is a deciduous climber from eastern Asia, specifically India and Burma, and is suitable for growing on shady walls, fences and trellis screens. It is also an ideal subject for a woodland garden, as the species grows in woodland conditions in the wild. It looks equally at home in a shrub border. This climber can be grown up large mature trees or over large shrubs, but this technique is only recommended for gardens in mild climates. Height 10m (30ft). Female plants produce small red berries, used in Chinese medicine to treat a wide range of ailments.

SCHISANDRA AT A GLANCE

A twining climber which has clusters of cream flowers followed by red fruits. Hardy to −15°C (5°F).

JAN	/	COMPANION PLANTS
FEB	planting 🌿	Schisandra associates well
MAR	planting 🌿	with shrubs and woodland-
APR	planting 🌿	garden plants
MAY	flowering ❀	
JUN	flowering ❀	
JULY	flowering ❀	
AUG	flowering ❀	
SEP	/	
OCT	/	
NOV	/	
DEC	/	

CONDITIONS

Aspect Grows well in either full sun or partial shade.
Site Moisture retentive but well-drained, reasonably fertile soil is recommended.

GROWING METHOD

Propagation Sow seeds as soon as collected in the autumn and germinate them in a cold frame. Take semi-ripe cuttings in summer.
Watering Apply water if the soil starts to dry out excessively during the summer.
Feeding Apply a slow-release fertilizer, such as the organic blood, fish and bone, in the spring.
Problems Schisandra is not troubled by pests or diseases.

FLOWERING/FOLIAGE

Flowers Fragrant cream flowers are carried in clusters. Female plants produce red fruits in pendulous spikes. You will need to grow a male plant close by for fruit production to take place.
Foliage The elliptical leaves are deep green and shiny.

PRUNING

Requirements No regular pruning needed but cut back any overlong or badly placed shoots to within several buds of the main stems. You can also cut back shoots to keep the plant within its allotted space. Renovation may be needed after some years, cutting the oldest stems down to the ground. This is best done over a few years to prevent too much loss of flower. Pruning is carried out in late winter or early spring.

SCHIZOPHRAGMA
Schizophragma

SCHIZOPHRAGMA HYDRANGEOIDES *has plenty to shout about, with rich green leaves in season and ebullient white blooms.*

IN THE SUMMER, S. hydrangeoides *is a seething mass of pleasant white flowers, so densely packed that the foliage is hardly visible.*

FEATURES

Self-clinging climber

Schizophragma hydrangeoides is a deciduous climber from Japan and Korea, related to the climbing hydrangea (see page 87), and supporting itself by means of aerial roots. It is a lofty climber, growing up to 12m (40ft) tall, so it preferably needs a high wall or fence. Alternatively grow it through a large tree, or use it as ground cover, for example in a woodland garden or shrub border. This climber is grown mainly for its unusual and conspicuous heads of flowers produced in summer, but the foliage is also attractive and covers its support well. There is one other species in the genus, *S. integrifolium*, which is not quite so hardy.

SCHIZOPHRAGMA AT A GLANCE

A self-clinging climber with large flat heads of cream flowers surrounded by conspicuous bracts. Hardy to –15°C (5°F).

JAN	/	RECOMMENDED VARIETIES
FEB	/	*S. h.* 'Moonlight' has variegated
MAR	planting 🌱	foliage.
APR	planting 🌱	*S. h.* 'Roseum' has rose-tinted
MAY	/	bracts.
JUN	/	
JULY	flowering ✽	
AUG	flowering ✽	
SEP	/	
OCT	/	
NOV	/	
DEC	/	

CONDITIONS

Aspect A good choice of plant for partial shade but it also grows well in full sun. Must be well sheltered from cold drying winds.

Site Well-drained yet moisture-retentive soil that contains plenty of humus.

GROWING METHOD

Propagation Take semi-ripe cuttings in summer. Sow seeds in autumn and stratify over winter.

Watering Do not let the plant suffer from lack of moisture, so water well if the soil starts to dry out in summer.

Feeding An annual spring application of slow-release fertilizer such as the organic blood, fish and bone will keep the plant going all season.

Problems This climber is not usually troubled by pests or diseases.

FLOWERING/FOLIAGE

Flowers Flat heads of cream flowers with large oval bracts of the same colour around the edge.

Foliage The large, oval, deep green leaves are attractive in season.

PRUNING

Requirements No regular pruning needed. If necessary, after flowering, cut back by about two-thirds any overlong shoots and trim the plant to fit the available space.

SOLANUM
Potato tree, Potato vine

THESE DAINTY FLOWERS belie the vigour of Solanum crispum.
It may put forth flowers over many months of the summer.

THE POTATO VINE, S. jasminoides, *here in its cultivar 'Album',
is a half-hardy climber, needing conservatory protection in most areas.*

FEATURES

Scramblers

Two evergreen or partially evergreen species of this genus are generally grown. Both of these are very vigorous, growing to 6m (20ft) tall. *Solanum crispum* (Chilean potato tree) from Chile and Peru has fragrant blue flowers in the summer. The cultivar 'Glasnevin', with purple-blue flowers, is more widely grown than the species. The Chilean potato tree can be grown on a wall or fence, or used to cover an unsightly outbuilding. *S. jasminoides* (Potato vine) is a half-hardy climber originating from the jungles of Brazil and will need the protection of a cool conservatory in most areas. In the garden it must have a very well sheltered sunny wall. It bears scented, pale blue flower in summer and autumn. Both species can be grown as standards.

SOLANUM AT A GLANCE

Vigorous scrambling climbers with clusters of potato-like flowers.
S. crispum is hardy to −5°C (23°F), *S. jasminoides* to 0°C (32°F).

JAN	/	COMPANION PLANTS
FEB	/	Solanums look lovely with
MAR	/	red or pink climbing or
APR	planting 🌱	rambler roses
MAY	planting 🌱	
JUN	flowering ❀	
JULY	flowering ❀	
AUG	flowering ❀	
SEP	flowering ❀	
OCT	/	
NOV	/	
DEC	/	

CONDITIONS

Aspect	These plants need a warm, very sheltered position in full sun.
Site	Well-drained yet moisture-retentive, reasonably fertile soil, ideally slightly alkaline.

GROWING METHOD

Propagation	Take semi-ripe cuttings in summer.
Watering	Water only if the soil starts to dry out excessively in the summer.
Feeding	An annual application of slow-release fertilizer such as blood, fish and bone, preferably in the spring, will be sufficient.
Problems	Plants are prone to attacks from aphids.

FLOWERING/FOLIAGE

Flowers	Produces large clusters of potato-like (star-shaped) flowers.
Foliage	The deep green oval leaves of these plants are not particularly attractive.

PRUNING

Requirements Solanums flower on the current year's shoots. Train a permanent framework of stems and spur prune back to this in early spring each year by cutting back lateral shoots to within two or three buds of the main stems. Also prune the plant back to fit the available space. Renovation pruning is not recommended – better to replace overgrown plants. Wear gloves when pruning as the sap can cause an allergic reaction in some people.

STAUNTONIA HEXAPHYLLA
Stauntonia

JUST AS IN its natural habitat in Japan and south Korea, this Stauntonia hexaphylla *has found a tree to twine its way around.*

ALTHOUGH IT DOES produce attractive flowers, S. hexaphylla *is also grown for its pleasant, lush, evergreen foliage.*

FEATURES

Twiner

This is a vigorous, evergreen climber from Japan and south Korea, where it is largely found growing in woodland conditions. It is related and similar to *Holboellia latifolia* (see page 85). Stauntonias are grown for their attractive bell-shaped flowers, which are produced in spring, and for their lush foliage that serves to cover their support well. Grow this climber on a sheltered wall or fence, or allow it to scramble through a large mature shrub or up a tree. Although this plant is frost hardy it will not survive severe cold spells. In areas that suffer from hard frosts it is best to grow it in a cool conservatory. The eventual height of this plant is 10m (30ft).

STAUNTONIA AT A GLANCE

A vigorous twiner with white, violet-flushed, bell-shaped flowers in spring. Hardy to –5°C (23°F).

JAN	/	COMPANION PLANTS
FEB	/	Try growing this climber
MAR	/	with spring-flowering
APR	planting	clematis.
MAY	flowering	
JUN	/	
JULY	/	
OCT	/	
NOV	/	
DEC	/	

CONDITIONS

Aspect	Full sun or partial shade, warm and well sheltered from cold winds.
Site	Stauntonia will get by in any well-drained soil that is reasonably fertile.

GROWING METHOD

Propagation	Semi-ripe cuttings taken in summer. Sow seeds in spring and germinate in a temperature of 16°C (61°F).
Watering	Water the plant well if the soil starts to dry out excessively in the summer.
Feeding	Feed annually in the spring. The slow-release organic fertilizer blood fish and bone can be recommended.
Problems	There are no problems from pests or diseases.

FLOWERING/FOLIAGE

Flowers	Pendulous clusters of scented, white, bell-shaped flowers, tinted with violet may be followed by edible, purple fruits (a male and female plant are necessary to obtain fruits).
Foliage	Deep green, shiny, leathery, hand-shaped leaves make a good background for the flowers.

PRUNING

Requirements	Spur pruning. To keep growth under control, shorten lateral shoots to six buds in summer, and then in early spring cut them back again, to within two or three buds of the main stems.

TRACHELOSPERMUM
Star jasmine

THE WHITE FLOWERS of Trachelospermum jasminoides *are enjoyed for their appearance as well as their strong perfume.*

THIS LUSH PLANT of T. jasminoides has been trained and pruned most effectively to echo the angle of the steps and then curve up again.

FEATURES

Twiner

Trachelospermum jasminoides is a handsome, evergreen, twining climber from China, Japan and Korea. It is valued for its pleasing foliage and for its clusters of strongly perfumed white flowers, which appear in mid- to late summer and age to cream through the flowering season. The blooms are reminiscent of the true jasmine (see pages 88–89). It is an ideal subject for growing on walls, fences, trellis screens, pergolas, arches and arbours. Star jasmine can also be grown as ground cover, for example in a shrub border, or used for covering a bank. Once established it grows quite quickly, and in maturity it reaches a height of 9m (28ft). In areas subject to very hard winters this climber should be grown in a cool conservatory or glasshouse.

TRACHELOSPERMUM AT A GLANCE

A jasmine-like climber with very dense growth and sweetly fragrant white flowers. Hardy to –5°C (23°F).

JAN	/	**COMPANION PLANTS**
FEB	/	A good companion for red or
MAR	planting ✤	pink climbing roses.
APR	planting ✤	
MAY	planting ✤	
JUN	/	
JULY	flowering ✤	
AUG	flowering ✤	
SEP	/	
OCT	/	
NOV	/	
DEC	/	

CONDITIONS

Aspect	Must be very well sheltered and warm. Full sun or partial shade are acceptable.
Site	This climber likes a good, reasonably rich soil that is well drained.

GROWING METHOD

Propagation	Take semi-ripe cuttings in the summer and then provide them with bottom heat – about 20°C (68°F). Carry out serpentine layering in the spring.
Watering	Do not let the star jasmine suffer from lack of moisture. Water well in summer if the soil starts to become excessively dry.
Feeding	Give an annual spring application of slow-release fertilizer, such as blood, fish and bone.
Problems	There are no problems from pests or diseases.

FLOWERING/FOLIAGE

Flowers	Clusters of white, star-shaped, highly fragrant flowers reminiscent of jasmine.
Foliage	Deep green, shiny, oval leaves.

PRUNING

Requirements	Needs little pruning. In early spring thin out some of the oldest stems if necessary. Bear in mind that this climber is naturally very dense in habit so do not attempt to thin it out too much. Prune back the plant as necessary to keep it within its allotted space, but avoid hard pruning. It is best to replace very old neglected plants rather than renovate them.

VITIS
Vine, grape vine

THE LEAVES OF Vitis vinifera 'Pupurea' are purple in summer and become darker in autumn before they fall.

GROWING UP OUT of a bed, this V. vinifera 'Pupurea' adds a vertical element to the planting, and fills the blank space of the fence.

FEATURES

Tendril climbers

Apart from the well-known edible grape vine, cultivars of *Vitis vinifera*, there are several ornamental vines that are valued for their autumn leaf colour. *Vitis coignetiae* is a very vigorous species from Japan and Korea and is also one of the largest leaved. In autumn the leaves turn brilliant red. It reaches 15m (50ft) in height. *V. vinifera* 'Purpurea' has purple leaves in summer that become darker in autumn, and reaches 7m (22ft). These vines, whose summer foliage is also attractive, are ideal for pergolas, arches and arbours; also trellis screens, walls and fences. They can be used for ground cover, and *V. vinifera* 'Purpurea' makes a good standard for the patio.

VITIS AT A GLANCE

Tendril climbers valued for their large lobed leaves. Hardy to temperatures of −15°C (5°F).

JAN	/	**COMPANION PLANTS**
FEB	/	These vines look good with
MAR	planting	large-leaved ivies such as
APR	planting	*Hedera colchica* and
MAY	foliage	*H. canariensis*.
JUN	foliage	
JULY	foliage	
AUG	foliage	
SEP	foliage	
OCT	foliage	
NOV	/	
DEC	/	

CONDITIONS

Aspect	Full sun or partial shade.
Site	Any well-drained soil, but alkaline or neutral conditions preferred. Soil should also contain plenty of humus.

GROWING METHOD

Propagation	Take hardwood cuttings in late autumn or winter, rooting them in a bottom-heat temperature of 21°C (70°F). Carry out serpentine layering in spring.
Watering	Vines will tolerate fairly dry conditions but it is best to water them well if the soil starts to dry out excessively.
Feeding	Apply a slow-release organic fertilizer in the spring, such as blood, fish and bone.
Problems	Leaves may be affected by powdery mildew.

FLOWERING/FOLIAGE

Flowers	Trusses of tiny green flowers followed by purple or black grapes which, in the ornamental vines, are not palatable.
Foliage	Handsome, large lobed leaves.

PRUNING

Requirements	Build up a permanent framework of stems and spur prune annually in mid-winter. Cut back side shoots to within two or three buds of their base. During the summer any very long shoots can be shortened if desired.

WISTERIA
Wisteria

EVEN THE STEMS of this wisteria have disappeared beneath an abundance of bloom—and there is no foliage yet to distract the eye.

THIS WHITE WISTERIA has been trained along a wire frame. The cascades of flower make it a high point of the garden in spring.

FEATURES

Twiner

These very vigorous, fast-growing, long-lived deciduous climbers are desired by most garden owners for their spectacular spring display of pendulous, often fragrant flowers that generally appear just before or with the new leaves. The plants eventually develop thick stems and therefore are very weighty, needing strong supports. They are very amenable to training and can be formed into virtually any shape desired. Wisterias are often used to cover large pergolas, when the flowers 'drip' down inside in a very dramatic fashion. They can also be trained vertically along veranda railings or low walls. These climbers are often seen on house walls. Wisterias are ideal, too, for growing up large mature trees.

If you do not have the wall space or other suitable support for one of these magnificent climbers, then consider growing one in a tub

and training it into a standard to decorate the patio. Bear in mind that young wisteria plants can take up to seven years, or even longer, to start flowering, so patience is needed after planting. In the meantime, simply enjoy the foliage, which looks particularly lush when newly opened in the spring.

Probably the most popular wisteria is *W. floribunda* 'Multijuga', a cultivar of the Japanese wisteria. The fragrant lilac-blue flowers are carried in pendulous trusses up to 1.2m (4ft) in length. If this cultivar is grown on a pergola it is a truly magnificent sight when in full flower and the trusses are dangling down inside. It grows to a height of at least 9m (28ft). There are many other cultivars of *W. floribunda*. These include *W. f.* 'Kuchi-beni' ('Peaches and Cream') with its pink and white flowers, and *W. f.* 'Alba' with white flowers.

Also widely grown is *W. sinensis* (Chinese wisteria), with scented, lilac-blue flowers in trusses up to 30cm (12in) in length. It is a fast-growing and vigorous climber with dense trusses of flowers, growing to the same height as *W. floribunda* 'Multijuga'. Again there are numerous cultivars.

CONDITIONS

Aspect
Wisterias ideally need a warm sheltered site in full sun. Good growth and flowering are also possible in partial shade.

Site
There is every chance that young wisterias start flowering sooner in poorish or moderately fertile soil. If the soil is too rich they will tend to produce a huge amount of leaf and stem growth instead of focusing their energy on flowers. The site should also be well-drained yet at the same time moisture-retentive.

WISTERIA AT A GLANCE

Vigorous, deciduous twiner with long trusses of pea-like flowers in spring and early summer. Hardy to −15°C (5°F).

		RECOMMENDED VARIETIES
JAN	/	*W. floribunda* cultivars:
FEB	/	'Alba', white
MAR	planting 🖋	'Kuchi-beni', pink and white
APR	planting 🖋	'Rosea', pink
MAY	flowering ❀	'Royal Purple', purple-violet
JUN	flowering ❀	'Violacea Plena', double,
JULY	/	violet-blue
AUG	/	*W. sinensis* cultivars:
SEP	/	'Alba', white
OCT	/	'Amethyst', light rose-purple
NOV	/	'Prolific', lilac-blue
DEC	/	

THE DELICATE SHADE of this Wisteria sinensis *and the abundance of its blooms, make it a favourite in British gardens.*

WISTERIA IS particularly effective for framing windows, doors and other architectural elements. Blooms can be trained to droop into view.

GROWING METHOD

Propagation The easiest and most reliable method of propagation for the home gardener is to carry out serpentine layering in the spring. The stems, which are pegged down in a number of places along their length, should be well rooted after a year. Hardwood cuttings of dormant wood may be taken in winter, but these may prove a little slow to root. Once established, wisterias can go on to live for hundreds of years.

Watering Keep young plants well watered. Water established plants only if the soil starts to become excessively dry in summer.

Feeding Avoid fertilizers that are very high in nitrogen as they result in vegetative growth at the expense of flowers. Instead opt for a balanced slow-release organic fertilizer such as blood, fish and bone. One application per year, made in the spring just as growth is about to start, will be sufficient. Plants in tubs may need a further feed in the summer as plant foods are quickly leached out of containers.

Problems There are a few pests that may trouble wisterias, particularly aphids and scale insects. Also, a fungal leaf spot may appear but it is not considered to be serious. It shows itself as dark brown spots on the foliage.

FLOWERING/FOLIAGE

Flowers The flowers are similar in shape to those of garden peas, and in fact the two plants are related. Unlike peas, though, the flowers are carried in long, pendulous trusses. Blooms are generally fragrant. They appear in late spring and early summer.

Foliage Large, pinnate, mid- to deep green leaves are attractive in spring and summer.

PRUNING

Requirements Train a permanent framework of stems to the shape desired, then spur prune to this. Wisterias can be trained to virtually any shape, but on walls the espalier is a good shape as it has many horizontal branches. These flower much more freely than branches that are trained vertically. This shape also provides a stable base for heavy wisterias. The espalier is completely flat and consists of a single, upright stem with horizontal branches evenly spaced out on each side.

Routine pruning of established wisterias is carried out twice a year to keep new growth under control. In mid-summer cut back the new lateral shoots to within five or six buds of the main framework. Then in mid-winter prune them back further, to within two or three buds of the framework.

If renovation pruning ever becomes necessary, spread the task over several years, thinning out one of the oldest stems each year. Otherwise the flower display will be reduced considerably. The heads of standard wisterias are also spur pruned, in the same way as those grown as climbers.

Flowering chart for climbers

PLANT NAME	SPRING EARLY	MID	LATE	SUMMER EARLY	MID	LATE	AUTUMN EARLY	MID	LATE	WINTER EARLY	MID	LATE
ABUTILON				●	●	●	●	●				
AKEBIA	●	●	●									
ARISTOLOCHIA				●	●	●						
BERBERIDOPSIS				●	●	●	●					
CAMPSIS						●	●	●				
CHAENOMELES	●	●	●									●
CLEMATIS	●	●	●	●	●	●	●	●				
CLIANTHUS		●	●	●								
DECUMARIA				●								
FALLOPIA						●	●	●				
FREMONTODENDRON				●	●	●	●	●				
HEBE			●	●								
HOLBOELLIA		●	●									
HYDRANGEA				●	●	●						
JASMINUM	●		●	●	●	●	●			●	●	●
LONICERA		●	●	●	●	●	●					
PASSIFLORA				●	●	●	●	●				
PERIPLOCA					●	●						
PILEOSTEGIA					●	●	●					
ROSA			●	●	●	●	●	●				
RUBUS				●	●	●						
SCHISANDRA			●	●	●	●						
SCHIZOPHRAGMA					●	●						
SOLANUM				●	●	●	●					
STAUNTONIA		●	●									
TRACHELOSPERMUM					●	●	●					
WISTERIA			●	●								

INDEX

Published by Murdoch Books UK Ltd, 2001
Ferry House, 51–57 Lacy Road, Putney, London SW15 1PR

ISBN 1 85391 853 9

A catalogue of this book is available from the British Library.

SERIES EDITOR: Graham Strong

COMMISSIONING EDITOR: Iain MacGregor

EDITOR: Alan Toogood

PROJECT EDITOR: Angela Newton

DESK EDITOR: Alastair Laing

ILLUSTRATIONS: Sonya Naumov; Lorraine Hannay

DESIGN AND EDITORIAL: Axis Design Editions Limited

PUBLISHING MANAGER: Fia Fornari

PRODUCTION MANAGER: Lucy Byrne

PUBLISHER: Catie Ziller

CEO: Robert Oerton

GROUP CEO/PUBLISHER: Anne Wilson

GROUP GENERAL MANAGER: Mark Smith

COLOUR SEPARATION: Colourscan

Printed in China through Hanway Press

ORIGINAL TEXT: Margaret Hanks

All photographs by Lorna Rose except those by Tim Sandall (pp 4–5, 6, 7 bottom, 8, 9, 10, 11, 12 right, 13, 14, 15, 17, 18,
19, 20, 21, 24–5, 27, 28, 29, 30, 31, 34, 35, 36, 37, 38, 39, 46, 49, 50, 51, 54, 57, 60, 61, 63, 64 right, 65,
67, 68, 70, 71, 72, 75, 75, 76 right, 78 left, 81 left, 82, 85, 86, 88 left, 89 left, 91, 92, 94, 101, 103 left,
104, 106, 108 bottom); Garden Picture Library (pp 69 left, 79 right); Merehurst © (pp 26, 52, 53, 47, 58, 59,
64 left, 78 right, 84 bottom, 89 right, 90 left, 95, 100, 108 top); Harry Smith Collection (48, 56, 76 left, 79
left, 83 right, 88 right, 90 right, 97, 102); Photos Horticultural (pp 22 left, 77, 80, 83 left, 96 left);
A–Z Botanical (pp 22 right, 96 right); John Negus (69 right, 81 right)